Night of the Witches

© Marlene Raedisch

About the Author

Linda Raedisch writes and lectures on a variety of topics. She is a longtime library employee and professional crafts instructor who teaches classes on candlemaking, broommaking, and other old-time homemaking arts. She lives in New Jersey.

Night of the Witches

Folklore, Traditions & Recipes for Celebrating Walpurgis Night

Linda Raedisch

Llewellyn Publications
Woodbury, Minnesota

First Edition
Sixth Printing, 2020

Cover art © Bruce Hutchison
Cover design by Lisa Novak
Editing by Brett Fechheimer
Interior illustrations © Chris Down

Library of Congress Cataloging-in-Publication Data

Raedisch, Linda, 1968–
Night of the witches : folklore, traditions & recipes for celebrating Walpurgis Night / Linda Raedisch. — 1st ed.
p. cm.
Includes bibliographical references and index.
ISBN 978-0-7387-2058-6
1. Walpurgis Night. I. Title.
BF1572.W35R34 2011
394.262—dc22

2010038838

Llewellyn Publications
A Division of Llewellyn Worldwide Ltd.
2143 Wooddale Drive
Woodbury, MN 55125-2989
www.llewellyn.com

Printed in the United States of America

Contents

Introduction

> *We know that our forefathers very generally kept the beginning of May as a great festival, and it is still regarded as the trysting time of witches—i.e., once of wise-women and fays; who can doubt that heathen sacrifices blazed on that day?*
>
> —JACOB GRIMM, *TEUTONIC MYTHOLOGY*

Spring has come to the northern forest, but who is to believe it? No flowers bloom except for a handful of crocuses in hidden gardens and here and there a snowdrop. The buds of the ash are no more than tiny fists, the beech leaves not yet green. Above the treetops, the mountains still wear shining caps of snow. The evening wind blows cold as the breath of the frost giants, and anyone with any sense has already gone inside for the night.

Or have they? Just overhead, there is a sound like the rushing of crows' wings. A spatter of beeswax, still warm, glows among the roots of the beech, while high up in the

tree's barren crown, a scrap of cloth flutters against the stars. Can it be a coven of witches has flown over these woods?

In the clear light of day, such a thing would seem impossible. On any other night, you would probably swear that there was no such thing as a witch—at least, not the kind who streaks through the sky on a broomstick with guttering taper and billowing cloak. But this is no ordinary night; it is the thirtieth of April, the eve of May. Tonight is Walpurgis Night.

What exactly is it, this "trysting time of witches"? You may already have heard of Walpurgis Night's ancient Celtic sister, Beltane, when the cattle were driven through the purifying smoke of ritual fires and out into the summer pastures. You will almost certainly have heard of May Day, with its beribboned Maypole and flower-crowned May Queen. Walpurgis Night looks a lot more like Halloween than May Day. And where Beltane is fire and light, Walpurgis Night is *Sturm und Drang*: storm and stress.

At least, that's how it was represented in the paintings, poetry, and music of the German Romantic period. Eighteenth- and early-nineteenth-century artists like Goethe and Mendelssohn found inspiration in the native observance of *Walpurgisnacht*, and they, in turn, put their own stamp on the tradition. The poet Goethe's vision in particular has come to epitomize Walpurgis Night for many. But is Goethe's vision of wanton hags cavorting on a mountaintop the only one? By the time the Romantic Movement came along, the tradition had already weathered a number of artistic trends, religious conversions, cultural upheavals, and military invasions. Certainly, Walpurgis Night has always appealed to the dark side of the human soul. But *why* did Jacob Grimm's

forefathers choose to usher in the summer half of the year not with rejoicing, but with blazing sacrifices? And what should this night of witches mean to us today?

While this book will attempt to answer these questions, it will not tell you how to *be* a witch or even how a witch should be. If you already are a Witch, in the modern sense of the word, keep in mind that this book is not about you. It is, to some extent, about your spiritual ancestors, but for the most part, it deals with a product of the pre-industrial imagination.

If, on the other hand, you know little about witches, you may be surprised by what you will learn. For instance, not every witch was a pagan, and not every pagan was a witch. Not all witches were women, and many—if not most—of those accused of being witches were not witches at all. And hardly any of them wore pointy hats!

Those distant forefathers of Grimm firmly believed there were witches in their midst. Their opinions of those witches varied according to where they lived, when they lived, and what their needs happened to be. In the Norse sagas, one man's talented storm-raiser was another man's evil sorcerer. Even in the Christian era, the average villager might revile the resident Wise Woman one minute and ask her to cure his rheumatism the next. Accordingly, the witches you will find in these pages are sometimes helpful, sometimes hurtful, and often, like a storm cloud, simply unpredictable.

Rather than a history of witchcraft, this book is intended as a guide to the northern European perception of the witch as seen through the rather smoky lens of that witch's favorite holiday. And so, with guidebook in hand, let's join the witches on their ride!

One

Goodbye Bedbugs, Hello Spring!

The Druids called it *Beltane*, meaning "great fire." As much as the ancient Roman writers would have us believe that the cultural boundaries between the Celts and the early Germans were impenetrable, they were, in fact, not. Trends in metalwork, textiles, and even spiritual beliefs flowed freely between the two groups,[1] so it is not surprising that the date of May first, along with its eve, was of great importance to both.

Both Germans and Celts observed it by building bonfires and burning pungent herbs: fennel, rue, chervil, thyme, chamomile, pennyroyal, and geranium for the Celts; rosemary, juniper, rue, hemlock, blackthorn, and wild caper for the Germans. These smouldering bouquets of herbs also acted as powerful fumigants—something our forebears would have needed after a long winter with all the family, not to mention the sheep and the cows, shut up together indoors.

When the Romans pushed north into the world of the barbarians, they brought with them a festival known as the Floralia. As the name suggests, flowers were venerated at this time, but there was also a lot of drinking and dancing involved. The day also happened to be close to the hearts of Roman prostitutes. Pagans living under Roman rule may have applied aspects of the Floralia, which took place from late April to early May, to the old May Eve celebration.

In certain parts of eastern Europe, pitchforkfuls of burning hay were waved around on Walpurgis Night to impart the power of the sun, embodied by the bonfire, to the surrounding fields. In northern Scotland, village youths would dance round the fire, crying aloud for the flames to go abroad and burn the witches,[2] while in Germany the witches were said to be dancing round bonfires of their own.

Along with building bonfires, we know that the peasants of old liked to make a racket on Walpurgis Night, pounding the ground with wooden boards, blowing horns, ringing church bells, and, in more modern times, firing shots in the air. Noisemaking remains a time-honored method of driving out evil at important turning points of the year, such as New Year's Eve, and in the life cycle. An example of the latter is the tying of tin cans to a newlywed couple's car bumper. It is interesting to note that the moveable Jewish feast of Purim also occurs in early spring and also features noisemaking and costumed parades, not to mention the less-than-vaguely-uterine-shaped pastries known as *Hamantaschen*—all hallmarks, as we shall see, of the springtime fertility festival.

Through the ages, such springtime festivals have gone by many names and featured a subtly changing cast of characters. In medieval Europe, the night of April 30 represented Queen May's eleventh-hour bid to take back forest and field from King Winter.[3] Queen May, of course, was always the victor, but King Winter fought the good fight before he was driven off to the far northern reaches of his realm.

The dark hours preceding the triumph of Spring, or *Lenz*, as she was called by the Romantic German poets, were often marked by the burning of sacrificial victims. In later times, these were made of straw, in earlier times not. Our ancestors understood, perhaps better than we do today, that there is no such thing as a free lunch. If they wanted their crops and livestock to flourish, they had to offer something in return to the source of the abundance. Once these ancient farmers had secured the blessings of sun, earth, and all life-giving forces, they hedged their bets by weaving a little protective magic around their homesteads as well.

In historic times on May Eve, the Irish continued to drive their cattle through the cleansing smoke of the Beltane fires, while the Germans and English fixed talismans of fragrant herbs such as marjoram and gilly flowers[4] over the doors of their animals' stalls. Elder leaves, too, provided powerful protection against the forces of evil,[5] as did the prickly gooseberry and wild roses favored by the Bohemians.[6]

At this time of year throughout northern Europe, crosses made from the twigs of the magical hawthorn, rowan, and birch[7] were nailed to the lintels of both house and barn doors.[8] By the Middle Ages, the cross had become a Christian symbol but had not yet lost its association with

earlier beliefs. Those who made their living from the land had to protect it from disease, disaster, and the nastiness of witches. If the old magic could keep their crops and cattle safe, then the peasantry would not hesitate to use it, no matter what the church said.

As we shall see, Walpurgis Night was itself a manifestation of the equal-armed cross. Beltane was only one name the Celts had for May Eve. Their other name for it was Cet Samhain, *cet* meaning "opposite." This reminds us that it falls exactly six months after Samhain, the Celtic New Year—the holiday known to us as Halloween. Just as the cervix thins in the moments before birth, the usually impenetrable veil between the worlds is drawn back at these two important points in the year. At Samhain, the spirits of the dead were welcomed back into the family fold, feasted, and were invited to warm themselves by the fire. (This is, more or less, what trick-or-treating is all about.) As well as marking the beginning of the year as a whole, Samhain signaled the start of a winter that would last until Beltane arrived to usher in the summer half of the year.

To those who concern themselves with such things, May Day (May 1) and All Souls' Day (November 1) are known as *Cross-Quarter Days*. The Cross-Quarter Days are so named because they fall roughly halfway between solstice and equinox. There are, as you may already have guessed, four Cross-Quarter Days in all, the other two falling on February 2 and August 1.

February 2 was the Celts' Imbolc, the Christians' Candlemas. Candlemas marks the occasion of Jesus's presentation at the Temple and Mary's purification after giving

birth. In America, the date is better known as Groundhog Day. August 1 was a festival known as Lammas, a sort of abbreviation of "loaf mass." On this day, the first fruits of the harvest were dedicated to the powers that be—first the gods, then the church. Put-upon students of high school English may be able to tell you that Lammas is Juliet Capulet's birthday.

These, then, were the crossroads of the year. In classical times, actual crossroads were sacred to Hecate, Greek goddess of witchcraft. At a crossroads, the unwary traveler might see ghostly lights, hear otherworldly music, witness the dancing of witches and ghouls, and even lose his shadow. The form of the cross was a manifestation of conflict and change, an intersection of positive and negative. In Ireland and Wales, it was believed that if you sat at the point where two roads meet at midnight on Halloween, you might hear prophecies in the wind.[9]

In North America, Halloween is indeed the creepiest night of the year. This holds true even if you include Mexico, whose joyous, albeit macabre, Day of the Dead festivities begin the same night. In Europe, however, Walpurgis Night gives Halloween a run for its money at the very least. In England in 2003, hundreds of hopeful ghost hunters passed over October 31 in favor of May Eve to camp in the rain outside the paranormally active ruins of Tutbury Castle and there witness the thinning of the veil. (Two hundred reported that they had done just that, and of the several ghosts sighted, one even managed to draw blood![10])

As significant as the date has proven for ghost hunters, Druids, and Bohemian dairy farmers, Walpurgis Night

must now be ranked among the English-speaking world's lesser-known holidays. For the average American citizen, it rivals loaf mass for obscurity.

There is, in fact, no reason why the reader of this book should have heard of Walpurgis Night before now, especially if he or she has never visited one of those lands once covered by the northern forest: lands once rife with witches, dwarves, and will-o'-the-wisps. And if you have heard of Walpurgis Night, you probably have one man to thank for it. He is the poet-playwright Johann Wolfgang von Goethe, a man who, at times, lived very much in the world of will-o'-the-wisps and witches.

Two

The Brockengespenst and Other Tricks of the Light

Goethe's decision to set certain scenes of his dramatic poem/play *Faust* on Walpurgis Night has helped make the holiday's observance known to the wider world. The character of Faust does not much concern us here; suffice it to say that his legend grew up around a historical huckster named Johannes Faust who made quite a name for himself in sixteenth-century Germany. According to the stories, Herr Faust struck a deal with the Devil: his soul in exchange for magical powers, wisdom, youth, wine, women, song, and the demon Mephistopheles for a sidekick.

Immortality, however, was not part of the bargain, and inevitably there came the day of Faust's reckoning. In some of the stories told about him, Old Faust repents and is saved; in others, he ends up with his eyeballs stuck to his house wall.[1] Goethe chose the happier ending for his play, a work

that some consider his greatest accomplishment—it ought to be, too, for it took him several decades to complete!

At this point in any discussion of Walpurgis Night, it is customary to quote long passages from the related scenes of the play. I will not do so here. Rest assured that Goethe's *Faust* is indeed a classic, and should you decide to settle down and read it for yourself, your time will not be wasted.

As important as *when* Goethe set these scenes—the night of April 30—is *where* he set them: a barren mountaintop in north-central Germany. Goethe was a romantically minded young gentleman when he first scaled the granite heights of the Brocken, the highest peak in the rolling Harz mountain region. (It is doubtful that he had a will-o'-the-wisp to guide him as Faust does in the play, but who can say for sure?)

As Ireland is to St. Patrick's Day, so the darkly forested Harz is to Walpurgis Night. Let it be said once and for all that Harz does not mean "heart" in German; that would be *Herz*. Linguistic misconceptions aside, if you are into witches, it's hard not to heart the Harz. The mountains do not fall neatly into any one region but spill into the northern and central German states of Saxony-Anhalt, Lower Saxony, and Thuringia. Here, Nature has built the perfect stage set for the dark drama that is Walpurgis Night. At center stage, we have the Brocken, also known as the *Blocksberg*, or Block Mountain. The first written reference to witches gathering on the Brocken dates to the fifteenth century, but the precedent certainly goes back further than that.[2] In pagan times, which seem to have gone on a little longer in the impenetrable Harz than in the rest of Ger-

many, the summits of the Brocken and other mountains served as mist-draped altars of sacrifice.[3]

While Bertha, Perchta, Holda, and the other personifications of the old Germanic earth Goddess have now to settle for lighter fare, the blood of their ancient human meals has soaked deep enough into the granite that no amount of snow, rain, or sunshine has been able to erase the stain. It is not a stain you can see; it lingers in the form of stories. The snow, fog, thunder, and lightning that typify weather on the Brocken provide the special effects that keep the old tales vivid in local imagination.

If the Goddess's cult was not actually stamped out by Christianity, it was certainly heavily trodden upon. The old Goddess's priests were denounced as devils, her priestesses as witches. And so have they survived in legend. You can choose not to believe in such legends, but you might not want to say so out loud while passing through the Harz.

Take for example the story of a miner who, over drinks one night at the local tavern, scoffed at the idea that old women could climb onto broomsticks and rise to the tops of mountains. On the way home, he found himself surrounded by a coven of witches. It was Walpurgis Night, of course. One of the old hags decided to use the miner himself as her broomstick and rode him all the way to the Brocken.[4]

You might also want to refrain from snooping in the Harz. When one hapless young man spied his betrothed drinking a potion that caused her to disappear into thin air, he did what any sensible person would do: he finished off the potion and instantly found himself atop the Brocken

where his bride-to-be and a score of other witches were dancing with the Devil. When he confronted his fiancée the next day, she turned him into a donkey. The woman was not completely heartless, though. She eventually gave him the formula to turn himself back into a man, after which they married and lived happily ever after. We are not told whether or not they continued their visits to the Brocken.

Sometimes, the trip to the mountaintop was not made until after the trip to the altar. One suspicious husband followed his wife out into the dark of a May Eve to watch her disappear among a herd of wild horses. The husband was able to see through her and the other witches' disguises by plopping a bit of earth from the grave of an unbaptized child on his head. (One cannot help wondering where he got such a strange tip!) Picking his own wife out of the herd, he mounted and rode her into the sky. Apparently, he rode her too hard, for they both eventually fell to their deaths. Nevertheless, they still make the trip each year and are doomed to do so until the end of time.[5]

The Brocken provided such a perfect setting for the Witches' Sabbath that practitioners were drawn to its heights from as far away as France, Scandinavia, and the Netherlands.[6] Maps of the region from the 1700s show the flight paths of witches on broomsticks, hell-bent for the Brocken.[7]

Witches may visit only for the occasional Sabbath, but the *Brockengespenst*, or "Specter of the Brocken," is a year-round resident of the Harz. The Specter haunts the higher reaches of the mountains and, depending upon the powers of one's imagination, appears as either a simple cloaked fig-

ure with a rainbow or ring of light around its head or as a giant woodsman wreathed in oak leaves. He may even carry a pine tree in one hand.[8] In other areas of the world where it occurs, the phenomenon is known as an *anticorona*, or *glory*. It is, in fact, an optical illusion in which water droplets in the air form a tapestry of tiny mirrors, both magnifying the stricken observer's shadow and weaving bands of color around it.

The wooded stretches from which rise the Harz Mountains are darker and deeper than even the Black Forest. Hardwoods cover the lower reaches, while, farther up, firs and towering spruces provide fuel for Walpurgis Night fires[9] as well as cover for the accompanying revels. Archaeological finds show that hunter-gatherers had taken advantage of the bounty of the Harz for tens of thousands of years, but the first permanent villages date only to about the year 1000 AD because of the difficulty in clearing the land for farming.[10] The first recorded human occupants were the Harudes, whose name means "forest dwellers." Charlemagne declared the Harz a royal forest in which only he and his royal kin were permitted to hunt, and it remained so until about the middle of the thirteenth century.

How *did* the Harz become known for its witches? As Robin Hood demonstrated in England, one of the best places to hide from the long arm of the law was in the forest. In Charlemagne's Holy Roman Empire, merely to think heathen thoughts was a crime punishable by death. Those who had no wish to abandon their gods, and yet wished still to live, sought out the most inaccessible places in which to carry out the old practices. These daring nonconformists

may even have encouraged the stories of demonic doings in the forest in order to frighten away their Christianized neighbors. It took Charlemagne more than thirty years to at least nominally convert the intractable Saxons, but that was not the end of the war. When Pope Innocent VIII launched the *Hexenprozess*, or witch trials, in 1484, almost seven centuries after Charlemagne's death, he indicated northern Germany in particular as a hotbed of witchcraft.[11]

By the time the Brothers Grimm began collecting their fairytales, the Harz had long been acknowledged as a crossroads for the Wild Hunt and a meeting place for demons, kobolds, and Valkyries, as well as the more run-of-the-mill, broomstick-toting witches. To this day, the flanks of the Brocken boast such landmarks as the *Hexentanzplatz*, or Witches' Dancing Ground; a Devil's Pulpit; and a Witches' Altar.[12] The woods were even home to the ghost of a Thuringian nun, one Sister Ursula, later known as Toot Osel. A talentless chorister in life, in death she took the form of an owl, perhaps the native boreal owl that also goes by the Latin name *Aegolius funereus.* Toot Osel hoots mournfully to announce the coming of the Black Huntsman, as the demonized local guardian of the animals was known.[13]

Who knows what creatures, earthly or otherwise, the young Johann Wolfgang von Goethe met up with as he hiked through the tangled shadows of the beeches, then pushed aside the snow-laden spruce boughs on his way to the Brocken's summit. Though he made his own trip in December, he would have had no trouble picturing the witches gathered there on the last day of April to "dance, converse, concoct"[14] and stamp away the snow that is the old God-

dess's mantle. His poetic mind's eye would have seen them in their own dark cloaks, leaping the flames and whirling in the spring.

Three

From Fertility Festival to Children's Parade

While Faust helped greatly to publicize the tradition, it must be remembered that Goethe did not invent Walpurgis Night. It was, instead, the not-so-unique creation of ancient pagan peoples, with the Catholic Church pitching in its own two cents. Clearly, the Germanic Walpurgis Night bore some relationship to the Celtic Beltane and the Roman Floralia, but there is also the possibility that the ritualized revelry taking place on the Brocken originated in an even older culture.

Even the most ancient peoples have tales of Those Who Came Before. The dark forests into which the pastoral Celts and Teutons first strayed with their cattle, horses, and bronze cauldrons were not empty of human settlement. There were people already there, hunting, fishing, building pots by hand, and raising great stone monuments. These Stone Age folk may have inspired the stories of fairies and dwarves that have come down to us today.

We will never know what those first people called themselves or what name they gave to the observance of May Eve. Ironically, Easter, that highest of Christian holy days, was named for a pagan goddess, while Walpurgis Night, a self-consciously pagan rite of spring, was named for a Christian saint. There may once have been a goddess named Walpurga, Walburga, or something like it, but few references to her survive. We do, however, have numerous references to a Saint Walburga, an English abbess who was canonized on May 1. What better way for the church to subdue the old pagan festival than to christen it after one of its own?

Since the advent of Christianity, the old gods and goddesses have gone through a wearying series of costume changes. Once-important gods such as Odin and Frey became devils, Green Men, and Wild Huntsmen, while the goddesses, for the most part, were made over as witches. Even in the guise of witch, a goddess might find herself switching back and forth between two very different costumes: that of the horrible crone swooping down on her broomstick and that of the elfin princess who danced the snow from the crest of the Brocken.

Goddesses could also find employment as good fairies who presided over childbirth, spinning, and the growing of flax. Most of the time, they were helpful, benevolent spirits, exhibiting their divine rage only to shirkers and to those who forgot to invite them to their daughters' christening parties.

Time and the tide of belief transformed the erstwhile fertility goddess Bertha into, not a witch, but a far more

likeable White Lady, whose eyes were the vivid blue of flax flowers.[1] As such, she rocked the cradles of fussy babies and left gifts for good girls who got their spinning done on time. To those who did not, or who spun at forbidden times of the year, she showed herself in her more terrible aspect of big-footed, snaggle-toothed crone whose delight it was to set the offenders' distaffs on fire. If you were really, really wicked, she might take out your innards and replace them with straw![2]

In her glory days, the otherworldy Holda went by the name of Frigga. Frigga was the goddess who ruled over Valhalla at her husband Odin's side. In Christian times we find this erstwhile queen of the gods living in much reduced circumstances as Holda, a cave-dwelling hag. Holda was said to ride through the sky, much like a witch. She did not travel alone but was accompanied at all times by the restless spirits of unbaptized children. The fields over which Holda flew with her retinue would bear bumper crops in the fall, but woe to the farmer who snuck a peak at these unholden, or unholies, for he would be struck blind.

She appears in a somewhat more attractive light as the fairytale figure Frau Holle, or Mother Hulda. In the tale that bears her name, Mother Hulda showers a selfless, industrious young girl with gold, later pouring pitch over the girl's shiftless stepsister.[3] As mistress of the weather, Mother Hulda is particularly busy on the Brocken. The fog is her hearthsmoke, the thunder the turning of her flax reel, and the white feathers she shakes from her bedclothes the snow.

We have called it by the pretty names "fertility festival" and "rite of spring," but there may have been nothing pretty

about the earliest observance of May Eve. Much more than an excuse for dressing up, the occasion would have been marked by drinking, sex, and sacrifice. The officiants might even have put away a few magic mushrooms before they dispatched their hapless victims. In other words, the first Walpurgis Night, whatever it was called, was very likely a blood-soaked orgy, and that is the image that has clung to it through the ages.

Why such abandon? To better understand our ancestors' motives, it might help to take another look at Mother Hulda's weather trends and the cycle of seasons as they were perceived in the northern reaches of Europe. The longer the winter, the greater the people's fear that spring might never come. Something had to be done to ensure that the snow would melt, the ground would thaw, and that light and life would return.[4]

Among the Germanic peoples, the gods concerned with fertility were known as the *Vanir*. Their counterparts, the *Aesir*, lived in the sky and spent most of their time orchestrating battles. The cults of both might seem to us unhealthily preoccupied with sex and death. While the cult of the Aesir spent much of their time trying to predict and influence the outcomes of said battles, the priests and priestesses of the Vanir paid special heed to the womb of the earth and the dead who rested within it, for the dead were the source of the earth's fertility.

The departed had not really departed at all; they could still be called upon to impart visions and to bless the endeavors of those still living in an uncertain world. "As above, so below" was already a key concept in the ancient

fertility cult. The end-of-winter orgy, then, was a concerted effort to awaken both the dead and the new life slumbering in the barren ground.

Such efforts, however, had no place within the context of Christianity. What had once been viewed as a sort of sacred duty to party was now condemned as the "Witches' Sabbath" and strictly forbidden. There were to be no more gatherings on the Brocken, the church fathers ruled, no more sacrifices, no more telling fortunes or having fortunes told, no more tying and untying magical knots, casting spells, messing with the weather, or engaging in a variety of other activities in which the heathens may or may not have indulged.[5] "I don't believe in fairies! I don't! I don't!" the backsliding peasant might have protested to the early German bishops who had branded the very belief in fairies, witches, and the like to be an offense against God.

Fortunately, for those of us who continue to enjoy Walpurgis Night, not to mention for the Harz Tourism Board, old rites do not die out; they become cute. While lingering superstitions concerning witches, broomsticks, and the ringing of church bells are indeed now falling by the wayside, they will not be allowed to do so without a fight. Almost as soon as the church gave up its efforts to suppress the traditions of Walpurgis Night, even more effort was made to revive them.

In the early 1900s, a Walpurgis Society was formed in the Harz to keep the old festival going. But the days of cowering behind chalked crosses and bunches of herbs and waiting for the witches to pass by were over. Walpurgis Night was now to be an occasion of speechmaking and fine

dining highlighted by fireworks and the organized singing of folk songs.[6]

The next great change came after World War II, when the Brocken fell to the east of the Iron Curtain and could no longer serve as the focal point for West German festivities.[7] Nor were East German witches able to gather there after the summit was walled off and a radar station erected where bonfires had once blazed.[8] It was at about this time that the outdoor play and children's parade took center stage, often with a May Queen and black-clad Devil in attendance. While Wall and Curtain divided Germany, the influence of mass media began to blur regional idiosyncrasies in the West. The celebration of Walpurgis Night became one way for the villages to counter this influence. The coming of spring to the northern forest was greeted as an opportunity to promote and preserve village dialects and traditions through local performances and poetry recitations.[9]

Today, long before darkness falls on April 30, German children in kerchiefs, paper hats, and devils' horns stream from the village kindergartens, wielding broomsticks and plastic pitchforks. More and more, there are sprinklings of ladybugs and fairy princesses among the witches and demons. Once again, grown-ups can drink and dance by the bonfires on the Brocken, but it might be hard to experience either pagan ecstasy or medieval hexophobia when you know that just a few feet away there is a collection of winsome felt witch puppets for sale. (The presence of vendors on the Brocken is actually nothing new. Goethe's *Faust* includes a character known as "Huckster-Witch," who pro-

claims to the revelers, "Who'll buy? Who'll buy?—great bargains going!"[10])

Yule, once that dark time of year when the dead souls comprising the Wild Hunt passed over the frozen earth, has become Christmas, when children's stockings are filled with candy. Samhain has been tamed and renamed Halloween. So, too, has Walpurgis Night become largely the province of children.

And why should it not? In the festival's history we see mirrored the life cycle of the old earth Goddess it was meant to honor in the first place. Maiden, mother, crone: these are the Three Ages of the Goddess. Walpurgis Night, likewise, began as the sacred observance of a primal people. The agriculturalists who came after them called upon the sacred Mother on this day to bless the fields and pastures. Later, the medieval peasant defied the church by calling on the same deity in her incarnation as Holda, the crone, to pass quickly over his fields and banish winter in her wake.

The young girl who joins the village Walpurgis parade disguised in a white wig and her grandmother's shawl might imagine herself as a frightful hag, but in the very act of dressing up and taking center stage she is telling us that the old Goddess is young again. And her charms are not to be denied. There she is, preparing to throw off her cloak, to dance away the snow, and to coax new green leaves from the barren trees.

Four

The Good Walburga

As patroness of seven cities and protectress against witchcraft, magic, famine, rabies, plague, storms, and the common cold, St. Walburga is no one to sneeze at. We know more about Walburga's posthumous career than we do about her actual life, but this much is fairly certain: she was born around 710 in what is now Dorset, England, and lived most of her life under Benedictine rule. The idea that April 30 was her birthday probably arose after her death.

Walburga was the only daughter of King Richard of Wessex,[1] who some scholars maintain was only a chieftain,[2] and one Wuna, or Winna, who may or may not have been a queen. (King Richard the Lionheart is occasionally put forward as Walburga's father.[3] This would have been a neat trick on Richard's part, since he was born nearly four hundred years after Walburga lived and died!) Walburga's brothers were the saints Willibald and Winebald, of whose lives and missions their sister would later write. Her maternal uncle was St. Boniface, Archbishop of Mainz, who was given the unenviable task of Christianizing the Saxons.

At the age of eleven, this young English girl was entrusted to the Benedictine abbey at Wimbourne, not so much because she was believed to have a calling, but so the nuns could look after her while her father and older brothers went on pilgrimage to the Holy Land. Richard died of a fever a year later in Tuscany and was thereafter known as "St. Richard the Pilgrim." His daughter stayed on at Wimbourne for another twenty-six years.

In 748, Walburga embarked for Germany in response to her uncle's appeal for help in subduing those pagan Saxons. Her ship had not yet reached the mainland when the English nun was credited with her first miracle: calming a storm at sea.

The middle-aged Walburga was eventually given her own community of nuns at Heidenheim, in what is today's Baden-Württemberg in southern Germany. The name *Heidenheim* has been interpreted as "heathen home" or "home of Heido," a chief of the Alemanns, and was probably built over a former pagan holy site.[4] When Walburga's brother Winebald died, she took over the adjacent monastery as well.

Abbess Walburga died on February 25 of 775, 777, or 779, and was buried next to Winebald at Heidenheim. After the death of her surviving brother Willibald in 786, Walburga was gradually forgotten, her grave overgrown with the wild herbs that would later be burned to keep away witches on her eve.

The soon-to-be saint was rediscovered during restoration work undertaken by Bishop Otkar of Eichstätt in 870. At the behest of her own disgruntled ghost, Walburga was

exhumed and translated (i.e., moved and re-entombed) to the town of Eichstätt. The disembodied Walburga had complained bitterly of the disturbance of her tomb by Otkar's workmen, her supernatural ire causing one of the walls at Heidenheim to collapse. The poor bishop must have realized he would never complete his renovations until he had gotten the old abbess's bones out of the way. As it turned out, the move to Eichstätt would help keep the saint's cult alive, for Heidenheim fell to the Protestants in 1538.[5]

Benedictine nuns preside over Walburga's shrine to this day, collecting and bottling the healing oil that flows from her bones each year from October 12 to February 25.[6]

Several interesting legends arose around Walburga after her translation. According to one, the abbess had subsisted entirely on communion wafers and wine. Another tells of the miraculous recovery of a dying girl after Walburga prayed all night at her bedside. One of the most famous legends has to do with a lazy monk who forgot to light the torches one night at Heidenheim. Unable to find her way back to her chamber after saying her midnight prayers, the abbess prayed for light and was rewarded with a heavenly radiance. She also prayed for God to forgive the monk for his sloth.[7]

There are no contemporary portraits of Walburga, but later representations show her in Benedictine habit with a crown on her head or at her feet to remind us of her royal birth. The sixteenth-century Master of Meeskirch painted her standing within the pristine woodlands of Heidenheim, a golden halo behind her head and an open book in her hands. Walburga seems never to go empty-handed but carries various combinations of the following: crozier, holy book, glass

phial, scepter, and, especially in Scandinavia, one or more ears of grain. As a Benedictine of the eighth century, the real Walburga would have worn a long tunic of coarse black or undyed wool,[8] a practical garment that kept the cold out and the curves hidden, rather than the sumptuous blue and gold draperies in which she appears above her shrine at Eichstätt. Underneath her veil, the abbess probably kept her hair close-cropped, since free-flowing hair had long been considered the mark of the pagan.[9]

A few of the symbols with which she has become associated suggest that there is more to St. Walburga than meets the eye. As we shall see, the coincidence of her feast day with important events in the agricultural year demonstrate an identification with an earlier fertility goddess. Nevertheless, the earthly Walburga was a noteworthy woman both for and of her time. She was one of the first and one of the last abbesses to rule over monks and nuns together, for such "double monasteries" were prohibited beginning a few years after her death. As abbess, she would have been addressed as nothing less than "Your Majesty."[10] Her posthumous biographer, the priest Wolfhard, credits her with healing gifts,[11] so she may have been skilled in the use of herbs. She is said to have taken good care of those in her charge and to have worked for the enlightenment of the native women especially.[12] She has even been named as the first English and the first German author of the female sex.[13]

St. Walburga's ministry did not extend to the Harz, the region that would become most closely associated with her name. The northern Saxons were left instead to suffer the

depredations of Charlemagne, who attacked the native religion with a ferocity even greater than that he unleashed on the Muslims of Spain. The great king was taken to task even by his own Christian contemporaries for his treatment of the pagan Saxons, whom he corralled and executed by the thousands.[14] Had a more sympathetic agent of the church such as the Abbess Walburga been at work among those Saxons, the history of her feast day might have taken an entirely different course.

Walburga as White Lady

We can't say with any certainty how the Christian Walburga got mixed up with the fertility aspects of May Eve. It may have been the coincidence of her May Day translation with the ancient festival or the location of her original resting place in heathen holy ground. There is also the possibility that she shared her name with a Germanic deity. However it happened, the result is an interesting amalgam of goddess, witch, and saint.

Whereas the goddess Bertha/Holda often led the Wild Hunt, the Walburga of German folklore was pursued by it. In this, she plays the role of female forest spirit or fairy queen, rewarding those who shelter her with gifts of gold. Not content to keep to her shrine, Walburga spends the last nine nights of April fleeing from village to farm and on again, demonic riders at her heels.[15] Dressed all in white, with golden shoes and a golden crown, this Walburga has really let her hair down. Bearing both a spindle and a triangular mirror, she resembles the Norns of Norse tradition far more than her Christian namesake.[16] The nine nights connect her to Odin/

Woden, who hung from the World Tree for nine nights before rewarding himself with the gift of the runes.

We have seen the witch Holda flying over the springtime fields with her horde of unbaptized children, thereby causing the crops to flourish. Walburga was said to hide within the fields, sometimes inside the grain itself, and her passing was no less propitious. There is a widespread custom in Europe of fashioning the last sheaf, in which the maternal spirit of the harvest was believed to reside, into a human figure known in the British Isles as a "corn dolly."[17] In parts of Germany, this straw figure was named for Walburga herself.[18]

The folkloric Walburga's white raiment relates her to the White Lady, a more or less beneficent tutelary spirit. In the Middle Ages, the White Lady's appearance presaged the death of a member of a particular family, but she could also be a helpful local guardian.[19] Like all those spirits associated with death, she had also to do with the fruitfulness of field and family. And, like the white-clad Bertha, she protected the household, rocking the babies and keeping the servants in line.

The White Lady's French cousin, the Dame Blanche of Normandy, haunted narrow bridges, thorn-filled ditches, and river crossings. The traveler who wanted to get safely across had to dance with the Dame Blanche or do her some other service upon which she rewarded the traveler. However, if the traveler displeased the Dame Blanche, he was variously cast in the thorns, flung over a cliff, or abused by the cats, owls, and other creatures at the Dame's beck and call.[20]

Walburga's Symbols

Through the ages, St. Walburga has been pictured with a variety of symbols. The crown, crozier, scepter, and book are common to Catholic iconography, marking the subject as both an important woman and a Christian saint. The oil flask refers to one of the miracles ascribed to her after her translation. Other symbols appear to have nothing at all to do with the abbess, having been passed down from a long line of fertility goddesses and coming conveniently to rest in the figure of Walburga.

Oat Ear

In medieval European folklore, there is a widespread motif known as the "grain miracle,"[21] in which we can observe the age-old fertility goddess in action. In these tales, the goddess is identified as the French Queen Radegund or French St. Macrine, the English St. Milburga, the Virgin Mary, or our own Walburga. Whatever her name, the female protagonist is always in flight from some man or men who would do her harm. Her flight always takes her past a field where farmers are sowing oats. Soon after her passing, the oats miraculously shoot up and ripen. The rapacious lord, vengeful ex-husband, or troop of soldiers then arrives and asks the farmers if they have seen the sainted lady. The farmers reply truthfully that she passed that way while they were sowing the oats that now stand tall and ripe before them. The pursuer figures his quarry is long gone and abandons the chase.[22]

While these later saints were forced to flee on foot, the ancient goddess travelled in style. Both the Danish Nerthus—

who, as a goddess of both fertility and death, has been associated with Bertha[23]—and the Gallic Berecynthia were driven through the fields in well-appointed carts, according to the Roman writers. As it happens, we don't have to take the Romans' word for it, for the dismantled remains of such carts have been found in graves and peat bogs.[24] In those days, the goddess was equipped with much more than a mirror and a spindle; her priestesses' paraphernalia included such items as a red leather tent, a winged crown, adornments of both gold and bronze, and an assortment of splendidly worked vessels—one large enough to hold three hundred gallons of watered wine[25]—and a little stool carved from the wood of an alder tree on which the goddess incarnate could sit as she rode round the countryside, conveying her blessings.[26]

Walburga's tale differs somewhat from those of the other fleeing saints in that she asks the farmer to hide her inside a sheaf of already ripened grain. The farmer's reward is the grains of gold the saint leaves behind. Sometimes, Walburga hides among the sheaves on the wagon, turning the grain itself to gold. Likewise, the straw "Walburgis" figure that was woven from the last sheaf was often dressed up like a doll and brought home atop the harvest on the farmer's wagon.[27]

Celebrants may be surprised to learn that St. Walburga's official feast day is not Walpurgis Night nor even May 1; it is February 25, the supposed date of her death. Significantly, it is in late February that the fields are plowed and sown in the saint's adopted country of Germany.

In her earliest portraits, St. Walburga holds aloft a stalk of grain. To this day, Valborg, as she is known in Sweden,

holds three ripe oat ears. The grain stalk is much more than an accessory; to the peasants who lived directly off the land, growing their daily bread, Walburga *was* the grain.

Spindle

Urd, Verdandi, and Skuld. There may have been other, lesser Norns, but these were the three who held the reins, or, to be more specific, the rope, of fate. Their names mean "becoming," "being," and "that which will be," as in, "will be paid for," the price being the ultimate one of death.[28] Urd is always the first mentioned of the Norns. Her name, like the German *werden* ("to become"), comes from an ancient root meaning "to turn."

The Norns made their home among the roots of the World Tree, Yggdrasill. There they spun—each turn of the spindle an event in a person's life, each resultant thread representing an individual's destiny.[29] In the tradition of the Vanir, the Norns presided over birth, life, and death. The Aesir greatly feared them, for even the destinies of the gods were spun by the Norns. Yet unlike their Greek cousins, the Fates, the Norns did not just sit around spinning all day. In Iceland, they were believed to make the rounds of farmsteads—attending births, prophesying, and inscribing important dates into the woodwork.[30]

It is not surprising that the act of spinning should have taken on such spiritual significance. Anyone who has watched a hand spinner at work knows it is a rather mysterious process. Before the advent of the spinning wheel in the thirteenth century, European women and girls spent most of their waking life spinning. At home, at market, and all along

the way, they spun the fibers of wool, flax, nettle, hemp, and, in the case of wealthy women, silk. The goddess Bertha encouraged women in their spinning and was herself an embodiment of the flax. Walburga took on many of Bertha's aspects, so it is entirely appropriate that she should carry a spindle on her flight through the fields.

Mirror

The cauldron tended by the "weyard sisters" in *Macbeth* is a faint recollection of the Well of Wyrd, just as Shakespeare's three witches are seventeenth-century reflections of the Norns. In Norse mythology, the Well of Wyrd watered the roots of the World Tree, the great ash Yggdrasill. "Wyrd" is simply another way of spelling *Urd*, the Norn whose name means "becoming."[31] If you want to see into the future, you must look into the Well of Wyrd, or at least drink the water as the god Odin did, sacrificing an eye for the privilege.

Urd, Verdandi, and Skuld stand at the three points of Walburga's mirror. We see the Norns again in the three oat ears carried by the Swedish Valborg and in the triad of crosses that German woodcutters carved on the tops of tree stumps.[32] The forest-dwelling wood-wives were said to take refuge in the space inside these crosses when the Wild Hunt passed by. Like Walburga, the wood-wives dressed all in white and rewarded those who helped them with gifts of gold.

Although the well bears the name of only one Norn, the other two are ever present, for one must be in order to become, and all who become must eventually cease. Like Halloween, Walpurgis Night is a time for divination, to sit

in the greening wheat and listen for the whisper of destiny. If we could stop the fleeing Walburga long enough to peer into her three-cornered mirror, we would see ourselves not as we are, but as we shall we become.

Dog

Another of the goddesses with whom Walburga has been conflated is the lowland patroness Nehalennia. The name Nehalennia can be identified as neither Celtic nor Germanic, suggesting that she is a very ancient spirit indeed, long predating the Latin in which her votive inscriptions were written. Nehalennia's cult faded away after her sanctuary was overtaken by the sea in the third century AD, but she lives on, to some extent, in Walburga. There are, in fact, ecclesiastical references to a goddess by the name of Walpurga in Belgium, who was likened to the Roman Venus. Her cult was stamped out by St. Willibrord—not to be confused with St. Walburga's brother Willibald—in the early eighth century.[33]

What do these ladies have in common? Walburga is the patron saint of Antwerp and Oudenarde in Belgium and of Zutphen and Groningen in the Netherlands,[34] all within Nehalennia's old stomping grounds. St. Walburga's first miracle was the calming of a storm in the North Sea. Surviving inscriptions to Nehalennia thank her for granting safe passage across the water. Images of Nehalennia accompanied by ships' rudders as well as baskets of apples and other fruits suggest a connection to the Vanir and thus with fertility and the dead.

On eleven of the eighteen altars on which she is depicted, the goddess is accompanied by a very faithful-looking hound, another symbol of the underworld.[35] One of the banes against which St. Walburga was often invoked was the dog bite. According to her biographer, Wolfhard, the abbess often traveled alone through the countryside to tend the sick and was never troubled by the feral dogs that were at that time common in the wilds of Germany.[36] There persists to this day a tradition of leaving out bread with butter and honey for the "wind hound" on Walpurgis Night. To do so ensures favorable weather for the crops.

Oil Flask

When her tomb was opened in 870, Walburga joined the ranks of the *Elaephori*, or "oil-yielding saints." The oil, dew, or "pearls," as the secretions are known, were said to have flowed from her breast, and by the time of her exhumation had completely immersed her body.[37] Without taste or odor, the "oil" soon became famous for its healing properties.[38]

Since the ninth century, the regularly scheduled flow of Walburga's oil is said to have been interrupted only twice: once when the church was under interdict (i.e., Mass could not be said there) and once when thieves broke in and stabbed the bell-ringer, thereby polluting the site with bloodshed.[39]

Scientific scrutiny has shown Walburga's oil to be nothing more than water oozing from the stone on which the abbess's bones rest.[40] Scientific scrutiny, however, has no place in the realm of faith, and the Benedictine nuns continue to collect Walburga's oil in a silver shell, distributing it in artfully shaped glass bottles to believers throughout

the world. Quite likely, the stone and its secretions, like so much else, were sacred to the people of Eichstätt long before the abbess's bones came to rest there.

RECIPE: WALBURGA'S OIL

Fill a clear glass bottle with light, virgin (of course!) olive oil. Add a clean sprig of rosemary and let stand for a few days in the sunlight. The oil can be served alongside fresh white bread or drizzled over roasted potatoes.

CRAFT: QUILLED WINDOW ORNAMENT

The art of quilling was born in medieval monasteries as a way of using up gilded scraps of parchment. Hang these ornaments in the windows during the last nine nights of April, when Walburga and the little wood-wives are in flight. The spirits might even leave you a reward for sheltering them!

If there are children in the household, stock up on Hanukkah *gelt*—gold-wrapped chocolate coins—at the winter holidays, then make them magically appear on the windowsills at Walpurgis time.

For each ornament you will need:

- Three ½-inch-wide strips of quilling paper in green or another color of your choice. You can make your own quilling paper by cutting a sheet of construction or color copier paper lengthwise into ½-inch-wide strips.
- large needle, quilling T-pin, or rounded toothpick
- glue
- thread to hang it by

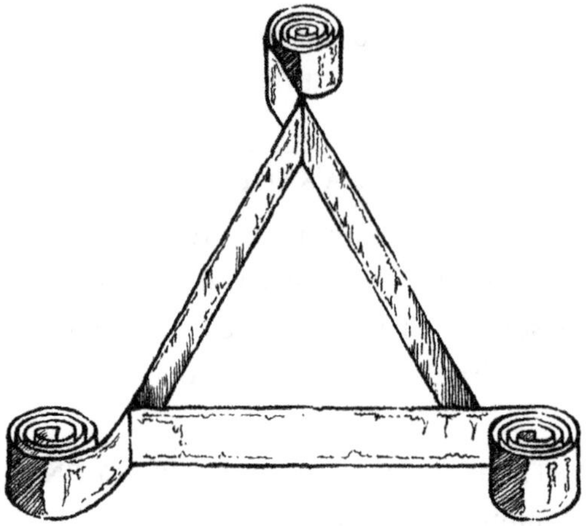

Roll each strip of paper fairly tightly around the needle, T-pin, or toothpick. It helps to moisten the end of the strip so it will stick to the needle. After several turns, you can remove the needle and simply roll the strip between your thumb and index finger. Stop rolling when you're about two inches from the end of the strip. Still holding the roll between thumb and index finger, let it unfurl slowly until you have a spiral about 3/4" in diameter. Put a dab of glue at the base of the spiral to prevent it unrolling any further. Repeat with the other two strips.

Assemble your three "fiddleheads" into a triangle by gluing the straight end of each strip to the base of the next spiral. The spirals should be all on the outside and swirling in the same direction.

Five

A Field Guide to Old World Witches

Otfried Preussler's classic German children's novel *The Little Witch* contains the following inventory of Walpurgis Night celebrants: "mountain-witches, wood-witches, marsh-witches, mist-witches and storm-witches, wind-witches, flower-witches, and herb-witches."[1] Much earlier, sixteenth-century witch-hunt opponent Johann Georg Gödelmann included *Unholden* (disciples of the goddess Holda), *Wahrsagerin* ("truth-sayer" or fortuneteller), and *Wettermacherin* (weathermaker) in a list of common terms for witches.[2]

By Gödelmann's time—the era of the witch-craze—the so-called legal definition of a witch was one who had entered into a voluntary pact with the Devil, who flew on a broomstick or other conveyance, and who went about her business under cover of darkness. This business was supposed to involve the killing and eating of children and the desecration of Christian symbols.[3] As powerful as this view was at the time, it actually enjoyed a relatively brief period of acceptance. The

witch as she survives in our folk and fairytales is, for the most part, not the product of late medieval law but a remnant from a much earlier belief system. The conversion of the northern pagan peoples to Christianity gradually impressed upon them the need to place the witch, Wise Woman, Good Woman, and forest entity within the context of a Christian universe.[4] But did she belong there?

The names *Unholden* and *Wettermacherin* are especially telling ones, for they demonstrate how, even at the height of witch persecutions, witches could still be associated with pre-Christian rites rather than anti-Christian deviltry. Witches were powerful women who could raise storms by shaking wet brooms over their heads or trapping spiders under pots. It was their own inherent witchiness that enabled them to do these things, rather than any affiliation with the Devil.

The earliest concept of "witch" in the northern European imagination was neither good nor bad but entirely other. A personified nature spirit, she existed both outside and independent of normal society.[5] Like many of the witches in the Grimms' fairytales, she does not necessarily set out to do evil; rather, she is crossed, offended, trespassed upon. She acts out only when her rampion is stolen, her house is eaten, or her invitation is lost in the mail.

I have included in this chapter both the Ash Wife and the Elder Mother, while putting the incomparable Mrs. Juniper off until chapter 7. All three are supernatural presences, certainly, but are they, strictly speaking, witches? What makes a witch a witch? Is she born or made? One answer may lie in the ancient and beautiful Croatian practice of burying women rumored to have been witches beneath

the roots of old trees. Rather than ascending to heaven, the souls of these women were subsumed by the branches shading their graves.[6] After a generation or two, tree and witch would have become indistinguishable.

What caused these women, in Croatia and elsewhere, to be called witches in the first place? It is possible that they were the descendants of priestesses who had followed the old gods by retreating with them to forest and moor. According to the *Ynglinga Saga*, the goddess Freya lived on after all the other gods had perished. She kept up the sacrifices to her dead brother Frey so that there would be peace and fruitfulness in the land.[7] Perhaps these forest-bound fairytale witches were disciples of Freya in her new guise of Mother Holda. Witch, priestess, primordial spirit: it is important for us to remember all of these on Walpurgis Night, to honor them and to respect their place both on Earth and in our own imaginations.

To that end, I have divided the witches in this chapter into thirteen tidy entries. Some entries are tidier than others. I had hoped to contain each witch in her, or his, own entry, but such containment proved more difficult even than trapping a *Drude* in a blanket chest. As you read, you will notice the Hag treading on the Valkyrie's toes, and the Valkyrie, in turn, stepping on the Drude's shadow. The *Alraune* seems unsure whether she belongs here at all or if she might be more comfortable in chapter 7, while the Cauldron Carriers and Cunning Men would probably prefer chapters of their own. Nevertheless, I have tried my best to make all of them stay put, to relate their histories, and to tell us in what form they may survive today.

Alraune

If ever a witch belonged in an herbal, it is the *Alraune*, for the name in German also means "mandrake." We will not delve very deeply here into the magical history of the mandrake root, for the Alraune is both less and more than the plant with which she shares her name. The "raune" part comes from Old High German *raunen*, "to whisper." *Raunen* comes from the same root as *rune*, denoting secrecy. The "al" part seems to come from *Alb*, one of a variety of troublesome spirits.

Associated since ancient times with incomparable powers of fertility and magic, mandrake roots were wildly expensive. Those hawked in medieval marketplaces were more likely to be the roots of the bryony,[8] gladiolus, or alpine leek[9] than *Mandragora officinalis*. These counterfeit roots were roughly whittled to lend them the human form that mandrakes were supposed to possess. A few inventive hucksters even wedged grass seeds into incisions made in the "crotch" to create a nice thatch of pubic hair.[10] On that note, in the old days, mandrakes were also known as womandrakes,[11] just as in German the name has both a masculine and a feminine form.

It was rumored that Dr. Faust possessed an Alraune, while Emperor Rudolf II owned two by the names of Maryon and Trudacyos. These specimens illustrate how even an emperor can be duped, for Maryon and Trudacyos were not mandrakes at all but the roots of the alpine leek (*Allium victorialis*).[12]

In the end, the magical importance the owner placed upon the figure mattered far more than its species. In fact,

the reverence attached to the Alraune may predate the arrival of the Mediterranean mandrake on the northern scene. For clues, we look to the tale of King Filimer, who, sometime in the mists of Gothic history (the sixth century BCE or before), conducted a primitive census, the result of which was the exile of an order of women known as the *Alrunae, Haliurunnae*, or some variation thereof. Apparently, these women had circled the wrong runes on their census forms, for they were all denounced as witches and driven out onto the steppes. There, they coupled with evil Scythian spirits and gave birth to a new race: those infamous sons of witches, the Huns.[13]

While the Haliurunnae were cast out, the figure of the Alraune persisted in both French[14] and German folklore, and also created a brief sensation in Tudor England.[15] The well-kept Alraune was dressed in silk and velvet, bathed in wine,[16] and fed regular meals of milk and cookies.[17] Peasants maintained her shrine in the kitchen cupboard,[18] suggesting that this root figure may originally have represented a household goddess or ancestral spirit. At her best, the Alraune could tell fortunes and even reveal the location of treasure,[19] but the Alraune who was not well cared for might shriek aloud and bring about the downfall of the family.[20]

Several girls' names have been derived from *Alraune*, though they are no longer popular. There was Albruna, a Teutonic seeress of the first century, and Ailrun, a swan maiden from the *Song of Wayland*. (Ailrun is depicted on one of the whalebone panels of the Franks Casket.) Much

later, *Alraune* became the title of a 1911 German novel as well as the name of its main character.

Ash Wife

Due perhaps to etymological confusion, sacrifices were made to the *Eschenfrau*, or "Ash Wife," on Ash Wednesday. The sacrifices were made not to gain her favor but to keep her from wreaking havoc, for the Ash Wife was nothing but trouble.[21]

As it turns out, we are all of us Ash Wives (or Husbands), for the Norse god Odin fashioned the first man out of an ash tree. Much, much later, the early church fathers went out of their way to forbid worship of the ash tree, revealing how its religious significance had survived into Christian times.[22] Witches continued to value ash saplings as the perfect shafts for their broomsticks. In pagan days, the Eschenfrau was very likely a neutral presence, like her sisters Frau Wacholder and the Elder Mother.

If you should find yourself in Oldenburg in May (more about Oldenburg under Wild Women), you may notice that there are no buds on the ash trees. This is because the Oldenburg witches gobbled them up on Walpurgis Night—a little snack to sustain them on their way to the Brocken.[23]

Bilwis

Yet another creature of uncertain category is the *Bilwis*. Over the centuries, the name *Bilwis*, or a variation thereof, has been used to describe a witch, an elf, a devil, and a bogeywoman. Originally a benevolent grain spirit, she was at some point

made frightening and co-opted to keep the children from trampling the grain. If the wheatstalks *did* get bent and broken, as from the wind, the finger was pointed at the Bilwis.[24]

A *Bilwezschnitt* was just such a swath through a field of wheat, oats, or rye, the forerunner of today's elaborate, pranksterly crop circles. The Bilwezschnitt was the work of a witch or devil with sickles bound to his feet. This kind of Bilwis, usually male, might be your own neighbor. Though most active at the summer solstice, the *Bilwis* with his swishing sickles was also known to appear on Walpurgis Night.[25]

The name seems to originate with *Bil*, a minor member of the Aesir clan. Bil appeared as a little girl and represented the waning moon.[26] The sickles on the Bilwis's feet may once have stood for the waning crescent moon. The Bilwis is peculiar to Central Europe—that is, those lands once occupied by the Celts. There is the chance that the name is actually derived from the Celtic sun god Bil, or Bel, as in "Beltane." Just as the Germanic gods would later be demonized by the church, the proto-Germans may have demoted the resident Celtic gods as they moved into Celtic lands.[27]

Bilwis also referred to a kind of elf that lived rough in the mountains and shot people in the knees with tiny, invisible arrows. Dirty children with tangled hair were sometimes called *Bilwis*.[28]

Cauldron Carriers

Contrary to popular belief, a warlock is not a male witch but, literally, an oath-breaker. A wizard is someone who is wise.[29] "Wizard" should be taken as a compliment, while

"warlock," among the Anglo-Saxons, was a deadly insult. Among the Frankish tribes, *chervioburgium* was not quite so deadly but still a serious barb. A chervioburgium was a man who carried a cauldron for a witch.[30] Of course, there *were* male witches, but among the Franks and other early medievals, they were not the norm. Magic, specifically the rather shady kind of magic known as *seid*, was the province of the goddess Freya. Women who practiced seid for the neutral purpose of divination were well-respected, while the men who dabbled in it were highly suspect.[31] Seid, it seems, was not an equal opportunity employer.

The Scandinavians believed magic to be a genetic trait. If a man had been born with a talent for prophecy or witchcraft, he could hardly be blamed for using it. King Erick of the Windy Hat was a renowned magician, and some Norse kings were even expected to do magic as part of their royal duties.[32] On the other hand, the sagas show us male witches both burning to death and drowning in large numbers, and not always at the hands of Christians.

The male witch's heyday did not begin until about 1500, and then it only lasted a few centuries. In this brief span of time, we find him making an acceptable living as a Cunning Man, a sort of anti-witch to whom locals would turn with their problems. Readers of Susanna Clarke's novel *Jonathan Strange & Mr Norrell* may notice some similarities between the fictional magician, Gilbert Norrell, and real-life white wizard James "Cunning" Murrell. Murrell was the seventh son of a seventh son, which probably had much to do with his choice of career. When he died in 1860, he left behind a cottage full of drying herbs, a "magic glass" or mirror,

a skull, and other paraphernalia as well as a chest full of magic books and papers. Alas, the books and papers have all been destroyed.[33]

Across the North Sea in Germany we find the *Hexenbanner*, a Teutonic version of the Cunning Man. A few Hexenbanner are still at work in rural Germany. This is not necessarily a good thing, for the persistence of the Hexenbanner means that women are still unjustly accused of being *Hexen*, of casting spells on their neighbors' cattle and causing other mischief.[34]

Drude

The *Drude* is not an easy creature to define. In German, a pentagram is called a *Drudenfuss*, or "Drude's foot," suggesting that the Drude leaves behind a birdlike footprint rather than a human one. *Drude* is occasionally interpreted as "harpy," which would explain the footprint but omits the possibility that a perfectly ordinary-looking woman can also be a Drude.

Like the nightmare or night hag, the Drude is a female spirit who oppresses sleeping people, livestock, and even trees. Certain women, for some reason, are destined to become *Druden* whether they want to or not, departing their bodies at night to fly around the countryside giving everyone bad dreams. Such women, it is said, do not enjoy themselves; they wish only to be released from their compulsion.[35]

To catch a Drude, you must place a bouquet of cowslips and other flowers inside a clothes chest. If late in the night you hear a rustling in the chest, you know you have

captured the local Drude.[36] Chicory, too, will guard against such hauntings.[37]

Jacob Grimm traced the Drude back to Throdr, one of Odin's birdlike Valkyries, who also survives in the name *Gertrude*. In Grimm's day, misbehaving children were often threatened with the *Drut*.[38] In Bavaria, Walpurgis Night is sometimes known as *Drudennacht*.

Easter Witches

Temporally, May Eve is not so far removed from Easter, so it is not surprising that one of Scandinavia's unique Easter customs should look so much like the German Walpurgis Night. It is a peculiarly Swedish tradition that attained its present form in the nineteenth century but probably goes back a lot further.

The average Easter Witch or Easter Hag is a little girl dressed up in a long skirt, shawl, and ragged scarf. While she almost always carries a broom, she may also have a copper kettle, coffee pot, or even a black cat.[39] (Boys are not excluded from the festivities; they dress up as Easter Trolls.) The Easter Witch behaves very much like an American trick-or-treater: if not appeased, she may commit minor mischief, or she may simply parade through the city streets with her classmates during daylight hours.

Today's urban Easter Witch looks more like Pippi Longstocking than a frightful hag, but back in the nineteenth and early twentieth centuries she still embodied the Swedish peasant's idea of a bona fide witch. The Easter Witches of old blackened their faces or wore bearded masks of papier-mâché and moss. Older and bigger, these witches

and trolls were capable of greater mischief and therefore had to be appeased with greater treats, including alcohol.[40]

Meanwhile, the real witches were believed to be active the whole of Easter Week. On Easter Eve (or Maundy Thursday, depending on what part of Sweden they were from) these nefarious females rose up from their chimneys and gathered in church towers, nibbling on the bells while they waited for their sisters to arrive. Then it was off to Blåkulla to celebrate with the Devil.[41] It is not clear what or where Blåkulla was. It may refer to an island in the Baltic, to the Blocksberg or Brocken in the Harz, or to a secret meadow reached only by magic means.

There must have been a lot to eat at the Devil's feast, for the witches often became wedged in their chimneys on the way back down. To prevent Easter Eve traffic in your own chimney, you could burn a sort of anti-"floo powder" composed of nine different kinds of wood. But don't light your fire too early the next morning or your neighbors will think you are a witch. Witches are always the first to light their fires on Easter morning, perhaps to brew up a potion for their hangovers.

Elder Mother

A member of the wood-spirit tribe, the *Elder Mother*, or *Elder Queen*, inhabits all elder bushes, and you may not help yourself to so much as a single berry without first asking her permission. Should you dare to cut down an elder without first paying your respects, then you had better watch out![42]

Elder leaves were fastened over the doors and windows on Walpurgis Night to deflect bad magic.[43] Jacob Grimm refers to the elder as the "elsbeer tree" and informs us it has the power to keep dragons from landing on the roof on this same night.[44] In the Hans Christian Andersen story "Mother Elder," the great lady herself appears among the branches of an elder bush that has bloomed out of a teapot where elder flowers are brewing: ". . . and in the midst of the tree sat a kind-looking old dame, wearing the strangest dress in the world; it was green like the elder-leaves, and with a pattern of large white elder-flowers spreading all over it . . ."[45]

Elder comes from the Old English *ellærn*, suggesting a possible connection between the Elder Mother and the elle-maids of Danish folklore (see Wild Women).

Hags

Just as the Alraune's identity is inextricably caught up with the mandrake, the hag has always been closely identified with her favorite haunt, the hedge—especially the hawthorn hedge. The words *hag*, *hedge*, and *haw*, the red fruit of the hawthorn, all come from the same root,[46] as does the German *Hexe*, "witch," and the Pennsylvania Dutch *hex*, as in "hex sign."

Hag, of course, is a not-so-nice name for an old woman. The loveliest young girl, if she lives long enough, will one day be a hag. It is a natural progression and one to which even the goddesses are subject. Bertha sometimes appeared as a hag, one foot grossly splayed from pressing the pedal on her spinning wheel. Likewise, in Celtic lands,

there were good hags who helped women with their spinning.[47] There were frightful hags, too, like the British Black Annis and the Highland Hag of Beare,[48] who was turned to stone each April 30 only to be reborn on Halloween.[49] *Hag* could also be a synonym for *nightmare*, the evil presence that causes bad dreams by pressing down upon and "riding" the sleeper.[50]

It is hard to say which was named first: the hag, the hedge, or the hawthorn. But the important thing to remember is this: the average hag enjoys turning herself into a hawthorn on April 30,[51] so unless you want to meet her, stay out from under the "hag-thorn," or any other hedge for that matter, on Walpurgis Night!

Valkyries

Brunhilda remains the most famous of the Valkyries, but there were also Finnilene, Friagabi, Gunna, Goell, Hloekk, and Skoegul, among others. The name *Valkyrie* means "chooser of the slain." At first glance, the Valkyries appear to belong wholly to those spear-toting sky gods, the Aesir, and not at all to the Vanir, the fertility gods residing in the underworld. Closer inspection, however, suggests that these indomitable female spirits predate the Viking Age distinction between Aesir and Vanir. They may even go back to the days when German and Celt lived side by side on the European continent, for the Irish sagas speak of goddesses who flew over the battlefield in raptor form, influencing the events unfolding below.[52]

The Valkyrie of popular imagination is a deep-bosomed matron who is often and incorrectly portrayed wearing a

Bronze Age helmet. Mead horn in hand, she welcomes slain heroes to Odin's hall at Asgard. This image comes largely from Wagner's opera *The Nibelung's Ring*, loosely based on the medieval German epic *Nibelungenlied*, which was in turn a distillation of the earlier Norse *Volsunga Saga*.

The Anglo-Saxons, when they crossed the North Sea, brought with them a more archaic form of the Valkyrie. Their *waelcyrge* were never glorified as were Odin's shining battle maids. The *waelcyrge*, rather, appeared as shrieking ravens and ravening wolves who hung about the dead and helped to lead that raucous procession of souls known as the Wild Hunt.[53]

Like the Vannic Norns, the Valkyries could decide an individual's fate, and they did so through the womanly art of weaving. *Njáls Saga* provides a graphic picture of these grim battle maids working at an upright loom. A blood-soaked spear serves as the heddle-rod that parts a warp of men's intestines. Human heads are the weights holding these horrible threads taut as the Valkyries shoot the crimson weft across with arrows, singing all the while of the deaths to come. When they have finished, they remove the cloth from the loom and tear it all to pieces. Each of the women, who are twelve in number, takes a fragment of the ghastly tapestry with her when she rides away.[54]

In the sagas, on the eve of great undertakings, men often dream of the "witch-ride" or of "witch-wives" holding such implements as a fork and a trough at the ready—ready, that is, to scoop up the dead.[55] Much of a Valkyrie's career, in fact, took place in men's dreams. In the Icelandic *Flateyjarbók*, a company of armed, black-clad dream women proph-

esy the death of Thidrandi as punishment for the household's recent conversion to Christianity.[56]

In the *Volsunga Saga*, Brynhild (a.k.a. Brunhilda) plays the part of both ethereal battle spirit and mortal wife. There may once have been a caste of women skilled in the arts of war and prophecy who served Odin on Earth. Just as the priestesses of the Vanir were driven underground by missionizing Christians, so would the priestesses of Odin have been denounced as witches. The fourteenth-century English poem *Purity* lumps together "wychez and walkyries" as all-around undesirables.[57]

Riding through the sky as they did, the Valkyries may also have functioned as weathermakers. This would account for the notoriously bad weather on the Brocken, for Jacob Grimm was of the opinion that Walpurgis Night had originally been an annual convention of Valkyries.[58]

Weathermakers

In her incarnation as *weathermaker*, we once again encounter the witch as force of nature. In addition to *Wettermacherin* and *Unholde*, the German witch was known as *Donnerkatze*, "thunder cat"; *Nebelhexe*, "mist witch"; *Wolkengüsse*, "cloud-gush"; and *Zessenmacherin*, from an Old High German word for "storm."[59]

Weather magic was particularly important to the seafaring Scandinavians. The Icelanders had a name for the raising of storms by magic: *gerningavedur*.[60] In the sagas, gerningavedur was the preferred means of confounding one's enemies and turning the tide of battle. The witches of the sagas were as likely to be male as female and they

were not necessarily evil. Their witchiness was an inherent trait, to be used for good or ill.[61] In the *Njáls Saga,* Svan of Svanhill, a skilled magician, conjures a ghost-ridden fog by swinging a goatskin and reciting a poem. (Oddly, this Svan eventually drowns in a storm-tossed sea.)[62]

German and Scandinavian witches had countless means of raising storms. The Unholden could cook up any kind of weather they liked using only three pitchers: one for thunder and lightning, another for hail and showers, and a third for cold, gust-driven rain.[63] Norwegian witches kept a variety of winds tied up in bags, untying the knots to release them as needed.[64]

Because it was injurious to crops, hail especially was thought to be the product of witchcraft. One Rhenish witch supposedly created a hailstorm out of her own urine. Her motive? Revenge, of course. She had conjured the hailstorm in order to ruin an outdoor wedding reception to which she had not been invited.[65]

Witches could also raise storms by trapping spiders under pots, shaking wet brooms, or dumping the foul leavings of their feasts into the sea. Once the tempest was in full force, they could throw lightning bolts down from the sky.

The association of witches with clouds may date back to the days of the Valkyries. A Valkyrie by the Old High German name of *Wolchandrut* ("cloud-drude") rode in a cloud, raining life-giving dew over the fields.[66] In the Old Norse *Lay of Grimnir,* we find another Valkyrie called *Mist,* which means just what it sounds like in English.[67] This association took a dark turn as the reverence for the Valkyries was converted to a fear of witches. In the nineteenth cen-

tury, peasants were firing their shotguns into storm clouds: hit the witch and you stopped the storm.[68] The weather-maker survives in more positive form as the fairytale figure Mother Hulda, who creates fog, thunder, and snow simply by going about her household tasks.[69]

The German witch could also summon fair weather, such as she might want to prevail on May Eve. To do so, she filled a man's shirt with oak leaves and hung it from a branch of a tree. The wind that arose from this charm would drive away the rain,[70] promising starry skies over the Brocken.

Wild Women

Wild Women fall into roughly two categories. The first comes to us from classical mythology and, ultimately, Mesopotamia. The archetype of the Wild Woman, and of witches in general, may have been Lilitu, or Lilith, the first wife of Adam. Lilitu, whose name means "belonging to the night," had the head and body of a woman but the wings and feet of a bird. Her marriage to Adam did not last, because she had a habit of sleeping around (though one has to wonder with whom) and killing babies (though one has to wonder whose). It was Adam's second wife, Eve, who stayed on to populate society while Lilitu fled into the wilderness. She's still out there somewhere, shrieking in the night.

Lilitu passed into Greek and Roman mythology as *Lamia*, a name that, in Latin, could denote either a vampire or a sorceress. By Renaissance times, *lamia* had come to mean, simply, "witch."[71] Like the *lamia*, the Wild Woman was at times believed to suck blood and eat babies.[72] She

was a follower of the divine huntress Diana and later of Holda.[73]

In spite of the horrible accusations, medieval and Renaissance artists usually depicted the Wild Woman with a pretty face and flowing tresses—and a shapely body covered in hair. At ease on the moors and in the forest, the Wild Women appear to be living contented lives. Paintings and manuscript illuminations show the Wild Woman posed with her equally hirsute husband, the Wild Man, nursing their hairy baby in a cave or wooded glade.[74] This Wild Woman is the antithesis of the civilized woman and, as such, neither good nor evil.

Like her classical sister, the Wild Woman of folklore could also go either way. She has many different names: *wood-wife, wish-wife, moss-wife, elle-maid*. Both the wood-wives and moss-wives tended to be hairy or overgrown with moss,[75] but the Scandinavian elle-maid was a glamorous creature. Long-haired and sumptuously dressed, the elle-maids liked to pop out of holes in the ground, offering bread and milk to children out herding sheep. Often, they tried to lure the children home with them.

The most famous Wild Woman of all may be the Fair Maid of the Oldenburg Horn. Her story is unusual in so many respects that it is tempting to believe it actually happened. It takes place, we are told, not once upon time but in 967 AD. The hero of the story, if he can be so called, is Count Otto of Oldenburg, who was out hunting in the heat of a summer's day when a lovely maiden appeared before him holding aloft a silver-gilt horn, and invited him to drink. The count accepted the horn but apparently did not

like the looks of the brew inside it. And so, with astonishing rudeness, he poured the contents out on the ground and rode away with the empty horn.

Eventually, both the horn and Oldenburg itself passed into the keeping of the kings of Denmark where they remain to this day. The story tells us that the horn already looked like an antique in 967 and that it was covered with all manner of mysterious symbols and inscriptions. The horn itself is something of a disappointment, for it is obviously of late-medieval workmanship.

Perhaps it is not the original. The only way to find out, I suppose, is to go to Oldenburg on a warm May day, after the witches have eaten the buds of the ash, and wait for the Fair Maid to come out of her hollow and offer you a drink.

Wise Women

The term *Wise Women* can be used to cover a whole spectrum of sorceresses, diviners, and healers. At one end of this spectrum, we have women like Veleda, a seeress of the Roman-era Bructeri tribe. Veleda was put up in a tower all her own, where she could prophesy in peace and counsel her people in matters of national importance.[76] Not far behind Veleda is the *Volva*, a practitioner of seid, the magical ceremony that seems to belong to the Central Asian shamanic tradition.[77] Eirik the Red's saga provides us with a detailed portrait of one Volva, a Greenlander named Thorbjorg.

There is no question that Thorbjorg is a witch born. All nine of her sisters had also enjoyed the gift of prophecy.[78] Like the Icelandic spae-wives who went from farm to farm

telling fortunes,[79] Thorbjorg spent the long Greenlandic winter on the move, offering her services to the cooped-up Vikings. Though there were a fair number of Christians in Eirik's Greenland, Thorbjorg is received as an honored guest.

She sweeps into the farmhouse in a floor-length, jeweled black cloak topped by a black lambskin hood lined with the fur of a white cat. Her gloves, too, are of white cat skin. On her feet she wears calfskin boots with knobbed laces, and she carries a gem-encrusted brass staff.[80] These are not just luxury goods to show off Thorbjorg's status; they are the ritually prescribed tools of her trade, as is the meal of goat's milk and the hearts of various animals that she is served.[81] In true shamanic tradition, the animals who gave their lives to feed and clothe the seeress will help her make contact with the spirit world.[82] The cat in particular was sacred to the goddess Freya, and seid, we are told, was Freya's own personal brand of magic.[83]

Thorbjorg is a haughty character, assured of her place even in a partially Christianized world. She is also one of the last of her kind. The Wise Women of later generations would not be able to afford jeweled cloaks and staffs or even knobbed shoelaces. As the church drove their rituals underneath the hedges, Wise Women would have to work quietly, accepting a meal or the gift of a few eggs as payment for their services.

At the opposite end of the spectrum, just where the rainbow is about to fade away, we find the Cunning Woman, or White Witch. Like her counterpart, the Cunning Man, she was able to hold out in the English countryside until

the nineteenth century by offering her neighbors protection from less-well-intentioned practitioners. Like the Scandinavian Volva, Cunning Women tended to be born, not made. *Cunning*, from the Old English *cunnan*, implied wisdom rather than vulpine cleverness. This wisdom was apparently passed through the blood, though not all family members received it. Though the position was hereditary, there was also a fair amount of training involved. White Witches learned how to use herbs, charms, amulets, and reflective surfaces [84] to diagnose and treat illness and thwart the magic of other, blacker witches.

Wolf Crones

A Swedish phenomenon, the Wolf Crones, or *Vargamor*, were old women—hags, if you will—who lived deep in the forest. Rather than turning into wolves themselves as did some members of the Norse warrior societies, they were sorceresses who could command the wolves' will.[85] Akin to the Vargamor is *Angerboda*, an old witch who dwelt in the ancient ironwood forest in Denmark.[86] Sometimes identified as a giantess, she is the mother of Fenrir, the wolf who will one day devour the sun.[87]

RECIPE: QUARKKEULCHEN

If there is such a thing as a flower-witch or an herb-witch, then why not a pancake witch? A Bedfordshire, England, newspaper reported in 1960 that in the springtime, children were still known to press their ears to the earth of a certain hill so they could hear the sizzling of the frying pan as the resident witch prepared her Shrove Tuesday pancakes.[88] I'm

not sure what recipe the Bedfordshire witch used, but here's one my grandmother used to make.

Quarkkeulchen is typical of the province of Saxony, where my grandmother grew up speaking Sächsisch, the local dialect. For a long time, no one in my family had a clue how to spell *Quarkkeulchen.*

Quark is a kind of fresh cheese that is difficult to get in the United States, so I have suggested alternatives.

Ingredients:

- 1 cup leftover mashed potatoes
- ½ package (3¾ oz.) farmer cheese—cream cheese will also do; if you want to reduce the fat content, use cottage cheese
- 1 egg
- 1 teaspoon lemon juice
- ¼ cup milk
- 2 tablespoons flour
- ¼ cup currants—the dried kind, which are not dried red or black currants but dried Corinthian grapes, and therefore a kind of raisin
- cooking oil
- powdered sugar

Cream the mashed potatoes and cheese together in a large bowl. Add egg, lemon juice, milk, flour, and currants.

Fry Quarkkeulchen as you would American pancakes. Dust with powdered sugar and serve. Unlike American pancakes, Quarkkeulchen taste good cold.

RECIPE: POOR HAGS

In Germany, French toast is called *Arme Ritter*, or "poor knights." Rich knights could afford meat, while poor knights had to make do with bread, eggs, and milk. Here, we adapt the knights' recipe in honor of Black Annis.

Ingredients:

1 tablespoon butter
1 egg, beaten
1 cup milk
5 slices anisette sponge, slightly stale
powdered sugar

While the butter is melting in the frying pan, stir the egg and milk together in a shallow bowl or baking dish. Add the sponge slices and leave them in for a minute or two, turning them over once, so both sides can absorb the egg/milk mixture. Transfer the slices carefully to the frying pan, pouring any excess liquid over them. Fry for about three minutes on each side or until they turn golden. Dust with powdered sugar and serve quickly to the hungry hags.

CRAFT: ORIGAMI KITCHEN WITCH

German kitchen witches range from simple whittled affairs to elaborately carved and costumed dolls. They all have the same function: to keep the pots from boiling over, the toast from burning, and to bring general good luck to hearth and home. Hang your witch in a corner of your kitchen and let her do her job. Unlike the more high-maintenance Alraune, the kitchen witch does not need to be fed.

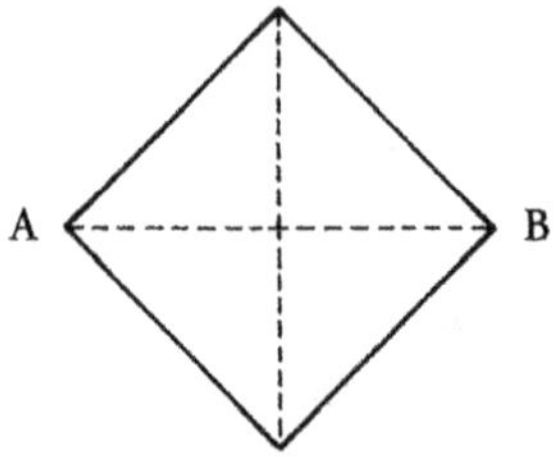

Figure 1

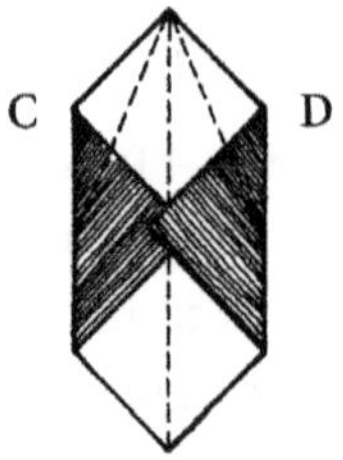

Figure 2

Figure 3

Figure 4

You will need:

1 4" x 4" sheet origami paper, black on one side and white on the other (a little larger or smaller is okay)

1 long party toothpick—the kind used to hold club sandwiches together

pine needles

string

small rubber band

1. Fold your paper in half, corner to corner, to make a triangle. Fold in half again to make a smaller triangle. Unfold all the way. The creases you have just made serve to mark the center of your paper. See Figure 1.

2. Lay the paper white side up and fold so that point A is slightly overlapping the center line.
3. Do the same with point B, so it is overlapping point A. See Figure 2.
4. Fold point C in to the center line. Do the same with point D. You have made the witch's pointy hat! See Figure 3.
5. Now fold the entire model in half lengthwise.
6. Use a dab of glue to hold points A and B together. These are the witch's hands.
7. To make the broomstick, bundle pine needles around the end of the toothpick and fasten with a small rubber band. Or, you can use string, fastening it as in the besom craft (see chapter 6).
8. Use the point of the toothpick to poke a hole through the paper just under the witch's hands.
9. Attach a piece of string at the witch's shoulder and hang her up where she can keep watch over the cauldron. See Figure 4.

CRAFT: PAPER CRONE'S MASK

People have been making masks for almost as long as they have had faces. One of the oldest representations of a masked figure appears in a cave in France and shows what may be a shaman impersonating a reindeer. Anyone who has ever donned a mask will understand how the enactors of ancient rituals still feel themselves transformed into the actual spirits depicted by the masks.

It is at *Fasching*, or Carnival, time that Germany's medieval city streets are flooded with thousands of masked figures, but you will certainly see your share of scowling witches on Walpurgis Night. The following project is the quickest way of turning a maiden into a crone. Like the Noh masks of Japan, this very simple mask relies on the play of shadow to lend it drama.

You will need:

1 sheet 8½" x 11" printer paper, color of your choice. (Green will look really frightful, white will look stark. If you want to give your mask an "antique" look, use parchment paper or paint white paper with a wash of black tea.)

scissors

glue

yarn

For the crone's face, you will need to transform the rectangular sheet of paper into a square sheet of paper. You don't need a ruler to do this. Fold the short edge of the paper up to the adjacent long edge to make a triangle. Using one side of the triangle as a guide, trim off the leftover end but don't throw it away; you'll need it later for your crone's nose. See Figure 1.

Fold your triangle in half, then fold in half again. Then fold it in half once more, lengthwise, as you see in Figure 2, so that it looks like Figure 3.

Now, unfold the paper all the way. You should see many creases radiating out from the center point of your square. Our withered crone has seen many winters, so if you want to

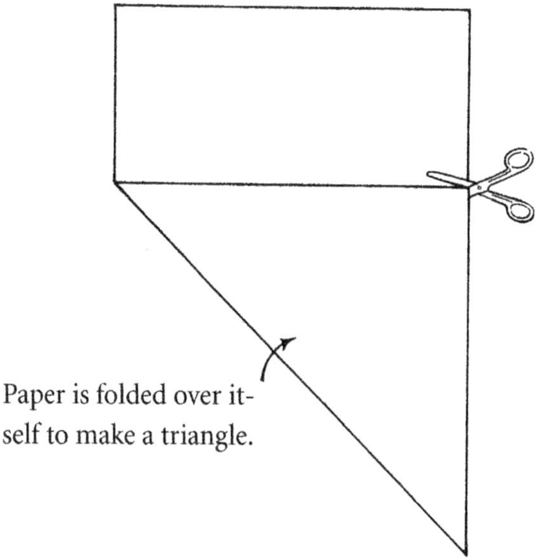

Figure 1

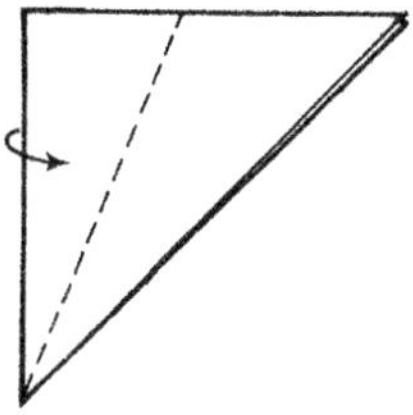

Figure 2

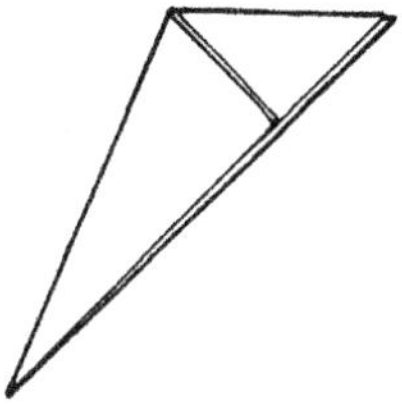

Figure 3

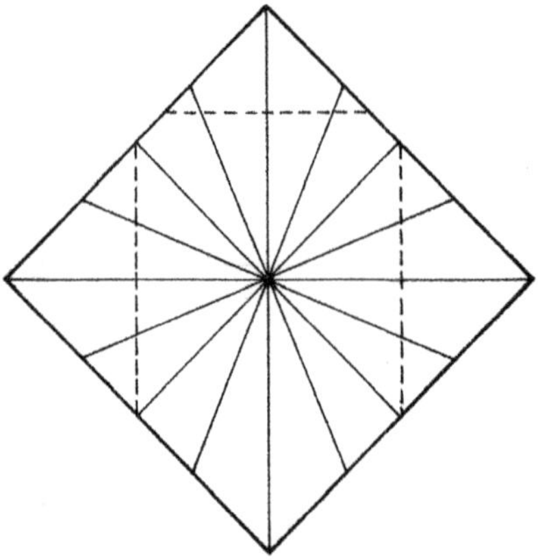

Figure 4

make even more creases, go ahead. Otherwise, fold along the dotted lines you see in Figure 4.

Your paper should now look like Figure 5. This is the back of the mask. Fold the mask in half lengthwise. Sketch an eye and half a mouth, as in Figure 6. Cut out the eye and

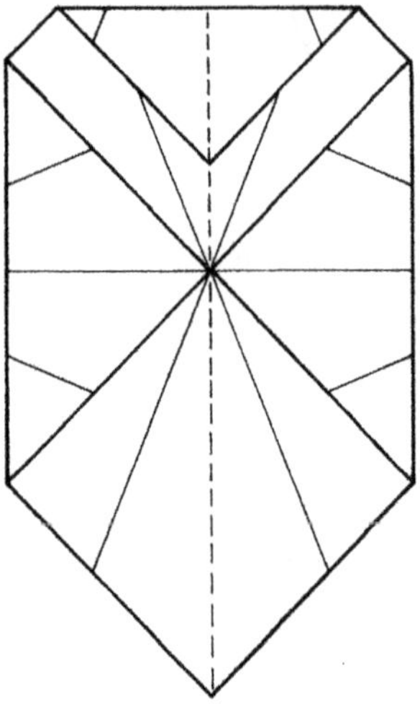

Figure 5

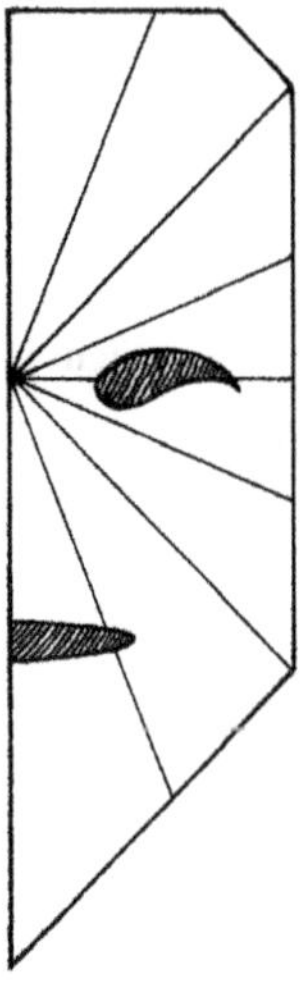

Figure 6

mouth and unfold to see the face you've made. Yes, your crone will have four eyes, but only two of them will show. The outer pair of "eyes" are for passing the yarn through to hold the mask to your face.

Now for the nose. Retrieve the end of the sheet of paper that you cut off way back in the beginning. Cut a square from the end. Remember: you don't need a ruler; just fold up the short edge! Fold this small square as you see in Figure 7 to achieve the kite shape you see in Figure 8.

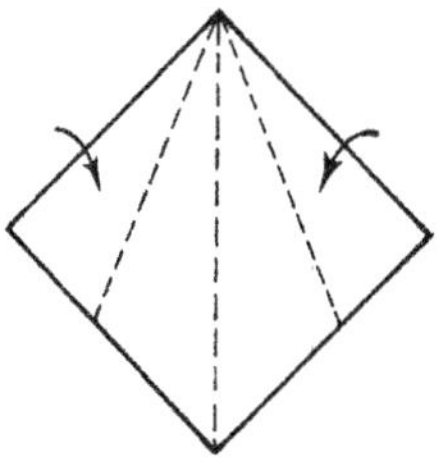

Figure 7

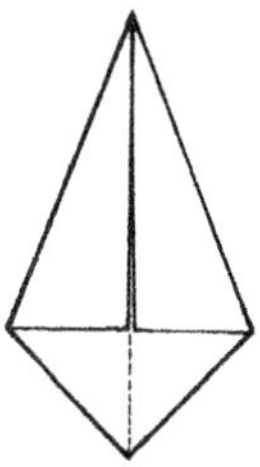

Figure 8

Slide one flap over the other and glue in place to make a very pointy three-dimensional nose. See Figure 9. Glue the bridge of the nose between the crone's eyes.

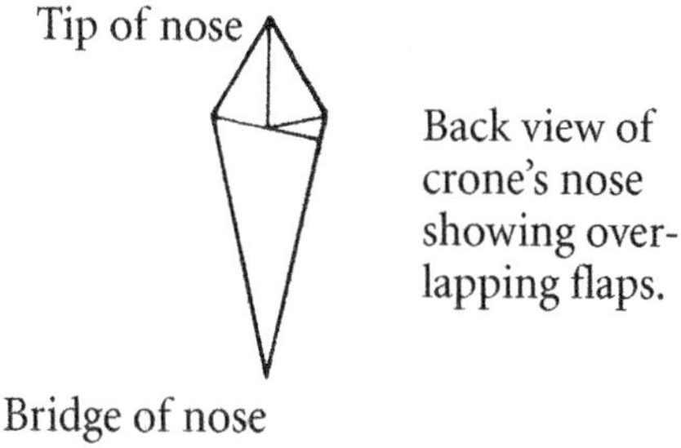

Figure 9

Your finished crone's mask (Figure 10) will look best when worn with a kerchief.

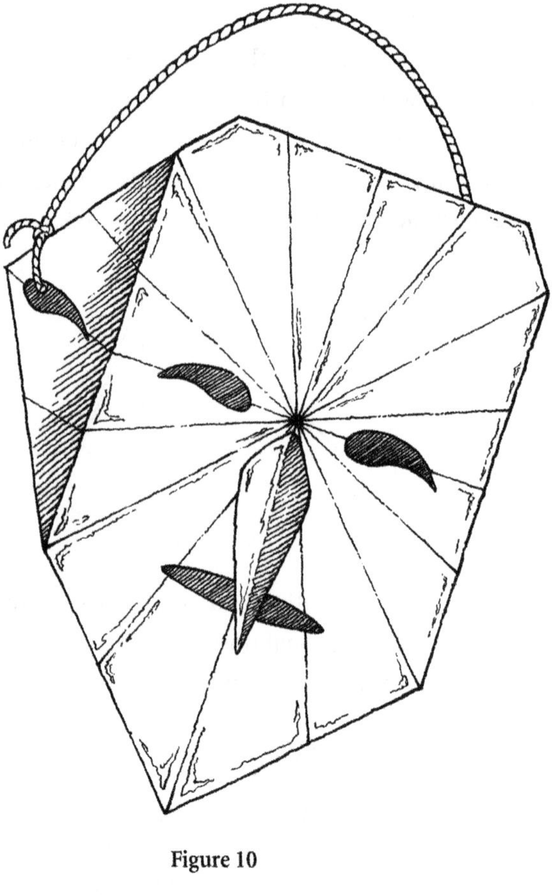

Figure 10

CRAFT: WITCH'S HAT

Imagine this: the bodies of three imposing women dressed in leather shoes and woolen gowns, each interred with what can best be described as a witch's hat. The hats were made of black felt,[89] one of them ending in a double point while another was so tall it had to be placed beside its owner in order to fit inside the grave.[90] The bodies of these women were excavated not in a European graveyard, but rather near the village of Subeshi in western China. Although the women died about 2,500 years ago,[91] the bone-dry sands of the Tarim Basin have preserved their bodies as well as any Egyptian embalmer.

The present inhabitants of the region look much like other East Asians, but these "Witches of Subeshi"[92] were of relatively tall stature with light hair and skin. They may have spoken a now-extinct Indo-European tongue such as Tocharian, but we cannot know for certain—the mummies aren't talking! Were these ladies the precursors of our modern European witches? It's hard to say, but their elaborate burials suggest they were held in high regard by their fellow basin dwellers.

The association of high, conical hats with wisdom seems to go way back. The Wise Men of the Christmas story belonged to a Persian cult whose priests, or Magi, wore tall, pointed hats. *Magi* comes from the same Old Persian root word that gives us our English word *magician.*[93]

Meanwhile, a handful of Bronze Age graves in northern Europe have yielded tall, conical hats made of beaten and embossed gold. But for all that, Old World Witches tended to wear kerchiefs or nothing at all on their heads. The black,

peaked witch's hat, like Halloween, is a recent American import. It seems to have been the artists of the Victorian era, rather than ancient tradition, who finally married the pointed wizard's cap to the Puritan's black, wide-brimmed hat to give us the witch's hat we know today.[94]

Nothing says Victorian like crepe paper and glitter! This sentimental witch's hat calls for plenty of both.

You will need:

- string
- 1 sheet newspaper or other large scrap paper
- 2 sheets black poster board
- 1 roll black crepe paper streamer
- tape or stapler
- glue
- scissors
- craft or utility knife
- black glitter (optional)

In order to make a witch's hat, you must first make a cone. One of the easiest ways to do this is to flatten out a party hat, then sketch that shape onto your newspaper or other scrap paper. A party hat is meant to perch on top of the head, while a witch's hat should sit comfortably and securely without the need for an elastic band. So, even if you are making your hat for a child, you will have to enlarge the pattern. Use a length of string to determine the circumference of your head. This is the length of the base of the cone. Add an inch or two, because the ends will overlap a little.

Sketch your pattern on the newspaper, cut it out, and try it on for size. If you're pleased, lay it on the posterboard

and cut out the crown of your witch's hat. Glue, staple, or tape the edges. You can hide the seam by gluing on a piece of crepe paper.

Set the crown aside and draw a large circle on the second sheet of poster board. This will be your brim. Use a large plate or platter to help you make the circle. Cut out.

Place the crown in the exact center of the circle and trace around it. Remove crown. Using your craft knife, divide this inner circle into eight wedges as if you are cutting a pie. Fold the wedges up and out. The crown should fit snugly over the wedges. Glue the points of the wedge to the inside of the crown. You may have to hold the points in place while they dry.

Now comes the fun part. Apply glue close to the edge of the brim. Unrolling your crepe paper little by little, glue it down, pinching it with your fingers as you go to create ruffles. The crepe paper should stick out a little over the edge of the brim. Create a second ruffle inside the first, just at the base of the crown. If it's still not fancy enough, dab the edges of the crepe paper with more glue and sprinkle with black glitter.

RECIPE: CRISPY WITCH SALAD

This recipe features a few dark, somewhat exotic ingredients to celebrate the earthy "otherness" of the witch.

Ingredients per serving:

Handful each:
purple basil
red leaf lettuce
blue-corn tortilla chips

pinch poppy seeds and/or black sesame seeds
honey mustard dressing
½ hard-boiled egg, sliced lengthwise

Put "greens" on the plate, arranging tortilla chips around the edge. Drizzle with honey mustard dressing, sprinkle on the seeds. Lay the ½ egg on top, yoke side up, so it seems to be looking at you.

Six

A Bit about Brooms (and How to Make One)

Through the ages, witches have been rumored to use goats, horses, wolves, pigs, pitchforks, baking forks, shovels, eggshells, and even unwilling gentlemen to get them up in the air and off to the Brocken. But none of these say "witch" quite like an old-fashioned twig broom, or besom. This was quite literally true in East Anglia, in England, where the term *besom* was synonymous with "crotchety old woman,"[1] and in Normandy, where a local term for a witch was *scobace*, meaning "woman with a broom."[2] The German term *alte Besen* translates as "old broom," but applied to a person, it carries the same connotation as the English "old bag."

The broomstick, an obviously phallic symbol, was a shoo-in as a prop in the springtime fertility festival in which participants leapt over brooms, shook them, and rode them round the bonfire well into modern times. Despite its masculine form, the broomstick is a distinctly

feminine domestic tool; male witches, when they flew at all, were more likely to use pitchforks. In the days before answering machines, a housewife would leave her besom standing up on the front step or sticking out the chimney to let her friends know she was out. This led to the belief that witches ascended the chimney along with their broomsticks.[3]

The earliest depictions of medieval witches show them riding bristles-down. Flying among the vaults of the twelfth-century cathedral in Schleswig, Germany, is a painting of a wild-haired woman dressed only in a cloak. She is riding what looks like a thistle, petals down.[4] Then, in the seventeenth century, we see the witches riding with the business end of their brooms to the fore, often with a candle stuck fast among the twigs—the world's first headlight? The innovation was short-lived, for the next century saw the witch once again flying twigs-down, the better to cover her tracks.[5]

The Quintessential Witch's Broom

If the quintessential witch's broom is a besom, then the quintessential witch's besom consists of a bundle of birch twigs bound with willow wands and fixed to a shaft honed from a young ash. The wood of the magical ash tree was supposed to save the rider from drowning in the event of an emergency water landing. Primeval spirits tangled among the birch twigs helped to raise the broom in the air and keep it there. It is no wonder our ancestors associated birch trees with both witches and flight. The birch acts as host to a hallucinogenic fungus, which in turn causes a twiggy out-

growth known as a "witch's broom."[6] The willow was sacred to Hecate, ancient Greek goddess of witchcraft.

Anyone who attempts to make a besom—and it is worth a try!—will find that the ash sapling was valued for its straightness, as were the birch twigs, which are also quite supple. Green willow wands make a nice sort of twine, tightening their hold as they dry over time. Broom squires, as professional besom-makers are known to this day, have also employed heather for the bristles and hazel wands for the binding.[7] Nowadays, besoms are often bound with wire.

Today's proud Pagan Witch might enjoy the symbolism of a besom made with heather, an evergreen plant that carpets the Central European moorlands. It is this humble shrub that gave us the word *heathen*. Most heather bears tiny purple flowers, but lucky is she who can find the rare white-flowered variety. While the German *Besen* refers to any kind of broom, speakers of Low German have a separate word, *Böhner*, for a besom made of heather. There's a lot of moorland in the Low German–speaking regions that, like the Harz, were also home to many heathen holdouts.

Be Your Own Broom Squire

Really, any straight branch will do for a handle and any straight, supple twigs for the bristles. Forsythia branches make good bristles as do pussy-willow wands. In North America, brooms were, and often still are, made of broom corn, which is not corn at all but a kind of sorghum. Collect two or three times the amount of twigs you think you will need and bind them together as tightly as you can. Feel free to use heavy twine or wire—Hecate will forgive you!

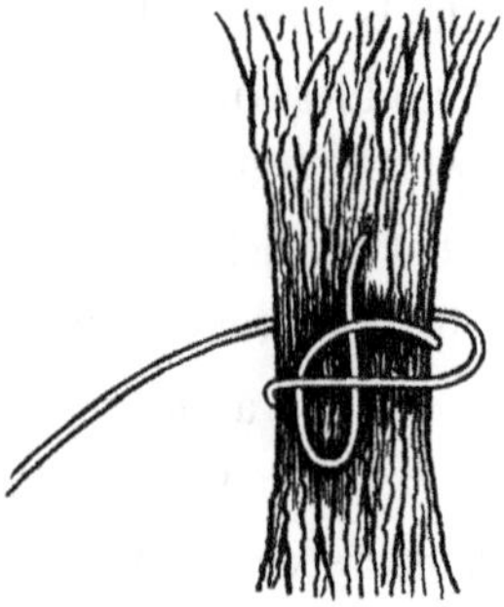

Figure 1

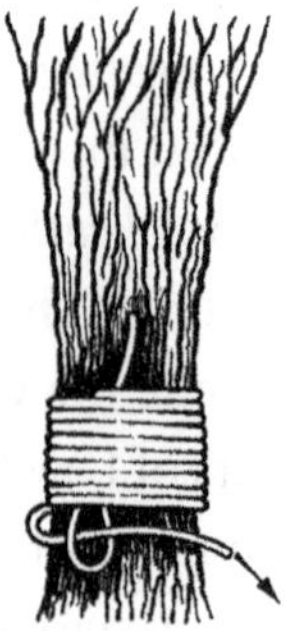

Figure 2

Figure 3

No knot is needed. Make a loop at the end of the twine, then wind the twine around the loop about ten times, very tightly, being careful to leave both the head of the loop and the end of the twine accessible. See Figure 1.

When you're done winding, pass the end of the twine that's in your hand through the loop, then pull the first end tight so that both loop and end disappear under the wound twine. See Figures 2 and 3.

Now, prepare the branch you have selected for the handle by scraping off the bark with a pocket knife and whittling to a point at the narrower end. Next, drive the pointed end into the center of your bundle of twigs. It should be a very tight fit. (As the shaft forces its way into the twigs, there will seem to be fewer of them than there were when you started, hence the need to gather twice as many.) To further tighten, wrap another length of twine around the twigs about an inch-and-a-half from the first.

If you want to make a really professional besom, then first drill a hole through the handle about a third of its length from the pointed end. When you've driven the handle into the bristles, the hole should be a little above the place where you've tied your twine. Prepare a wooden peg just thin enough that you can bang it into the hole and long enough that it will stick out a few inches, crosswise, on either side of the shaft. Bind the twigs again on the other side of the peg.[8] This will prevent the handle from shifting while you are "in flight."

If you have some birch wood at your disposal, you might want to try your hand at an "Indian broom." For this, you need a very sharp knife and limitless patience. Indian

brooms are made by scoring, then peeling back the fresh layers of birch wood ring by ring. This kind of broom was favored by the Algonquian tribes as well as by the European settlers of New England.[9]

A Few Words of Caution

We have said that just about any straight branch or supple twig will do for your broom, but certain of our forest friends should be approached only with extreme caution. For example, while Old World witches treasured the ash, even snacking on its buds on their way to the Brocken,[10] they despised the mountain ash, or rowan, whose red berries were used to work magic against them.[11]

Witches were known to take cover in elders, disguising themselves completely among the branches, so it is best not to cut down an elder lest you disturb the spirit sheltering there.[12] It was often an elder log that a witch tucked up in her bed when she went out flying. Hence the expression "I slept like a log."[13]

Hawthorn was also an acceptable wood for this purpose. And it, too, was a popular witch-haunt. Travelers were loath to rest beneath a hawthorn, especially on Walpurgis Night. On the one hand, hawthorn has been used to protect the home and to encourage lovemaking and fertility.[14] But if you make your broom of hawthorn, be careful never to bring it inside the house, for the presence of hawthorn indoors signals death. This may have something to do with the scent of its blossoms that, though the Greeks and Romans were fond of it, has also been compared to the scent

of the plague in seventeenth-century London.[15] The hawthorn used to be known simply as "may," and, indeed, the May King and May Queen were crowned with its snowy white blossoms on May Day. The subsequent sacrifice of said king and queen in ancient times may also account for the shrub's age-old association with death.[16]

No plant invites reverence quite like the yew. For one thing, it's deadly, something our ancestors learned long ago. Poison made from the nutlike seeds was applied to hunting arrows, while the wood has been used to make bows since the end of the last Ice Age at least.[17] The fleshy red "berries"—actually arils enclosing the seeds—are the only part of the plant that is not poisonous to animals.[18] The mournful yew has long presided over Christian graveyards, ostensibly to protect the dead from troublesome witches, but a few mammoth European yews may actually predate the foundations of the churches with which they are aligned.[19] Be sure to greet the yew in passing, but take nothing from it. You may prune a yew to help it maintain its dramatic shape, but do not bring the cuttings in the house.[20]

How about a broom made of broom? This yellow-flowered shrub was made famous by Geoffrey of Anjou, later called Plantagenet because he liked to wear a sprig of broom, or *Planta genista*, in his hat. A broom made of broom is all right as long as you put it away before dawn on May Day and don't take it out again until June. Sweeping a floor with broom in May invites the same kind of disaster as does a vase filled with yew or hawthorn flowers on the dining room table.[21]

More Broomstick Superstitions

Always store your broomstick twigs-up, and don't prop it in a corner unless you don't mind strangers dropping by.[22]

- A witch can summon a storm by shaking a wet broom over her head.[23]
- A broom stood upside down before a door will keep a witch away.[24]
- Throw a broom after a fisherman for good luck, but never ask a jockey to touch one before a race.[25]
- If you're not going to use it yourself, hide your broom away on Walpurgis Night or else another witch will commandeer it.[26] (The peasants of Silesia took this a step further, locking up anything at all on which a witch might ride to the Brocken on the big night.[27])
- Never burn a broom unless you're at sea and you need a little wind to fill the sails.[28]
- Never take an old broom into a new house.[29]
- Never sweep at night around a corpse or underneath a woman who has recently given birth.[30]
- Last but not least, never borrow a broom or lend your own to someone else; if brooms are anything like books, you'll never get it back!

RECIPE: BROOMSTICK BREAD

A few years ago, I was taking a walk with my Tante Erika near her home in northern Germany. It was August, and German schools were already back in session. Tante Erika suggested we drop by the local kindergarten to say hello to

a friend of hers who was teaching there. I had heard that German kindergartens were less academic than their American counterparts, but I was unprepared for the sight of twenty or so barefoot children zooming around the schoolyard, swinging from trees and baking bread over an open fire. They called it *Stockbrot*. Here, we call it broomstick bread. Simply take refrigerated pizza dough or dinner-roll dough, or prepare the dough according to your favorite recipe, and cut it into thin strips. Wrap each strip loosely around the end of a broomstick or another stick you have gathered outside. Hold over an open or fireplace fire about ten minutes or until golden.

Enjoy your bread warm with butter, red currant jam, or one of the following recipes.

Flying Ointment

There are many possible reasons why witches were believed to fly and why some women even believed themselves to have flown. Some practitioners, no doubt, experienced flight while in a shamanic trance, while others may have unwittingly been under the influence of lysergic acid contained in ergot, a fungus that invades the seed heads of barley and rye. According to Roman writers, classical witches could turn themselves into birds with the help of incense, a muttered spell, and a specially prepared oil—the recipe for which may have been passed down, witch to witch, over thousands of years.[31]

By the time of the European witch-hunts, the accused were purported to rub themselves and/or their broomsticks with an unguent variously composed of belladonna,

opium, hemlock,[32] henbane, hellebore, monkshood, bat's blood,[33] and the fat of children, cats, or wolves, depending on whom you asked.[34] It seems doubtful that anyone with a knowledge of herbs would have exposed herself to such lethal concoctions. The best result would have been a very bad "trip"; the worst, and more likely, result, death. The following recipes, on the other hand, are all completely safe.

For both recipes you will need one medium-sized mixing bowl and one smaller bowl lined with plastic wrap.

RECIPE: FLYING OINTMENT #1

1 stick butter, softened
pinch black pepper
½ clove garlic, minced
¼ cup fresh chopped dill
¼ cup chopped fresh parsley + 1 sprig

Mix all ingredients, except parsley sprig, in the mixing bowl, then scoop into plastic-lined bowl and chill briefly. Turn out onto serving plate and garnish with sprig parsley. You can cheerfully explain to your guests that the parsley is a stand-in for its own close cousin, hemlock, also known as "poison parsley."

RECIPE: FLYING OINTMENT #2

12 ounces soft, fresh cheese such as chèvre, farmer's cheese, or whipped cream cheese
½ medium-size red onion, chopped
½ cup fresh chives or green spring onions, chopped

Mix, mold, chill, and serve as in recipe #1.

ACTIVITY: FLYING LICENSE

Take your cue from the town of Bad Grund in the Harz, and offer your Walpurgis Night witch guests a chance to earn their flying licenses. Remind them to bring their broomsticks so they can complete the obstacle course you set up outside. Include take-off, landing, and parallel parking. Hang paper cutouts of birds from low tree branches and take points off for grazing them.

Once they've passed their "flying tests," the real challenge begins as they take on the DFB (Division of Flying Broomsticks). Here in New Jersey, we must prove our identities according to a six-point document system before we are granted our driver's license. As the reigning bureaucrat at your Walpurgis Night party, you'll create your own system to confound your friends. Instead of asking for birth certificates and social security cards, assign points to such articles as headgear (e.g., three points for a pointy hat, two points for a kerchief), black cats or other familiars, herbs, charms, or other amulets, etc.

Once the "applicant" has proven his or her witchiness to your satisfaction, you may issue the flying license. You can ask your guests beforehand to bring in small pictures of themselves. Better yet, set up a picture-taking station with digital camera, computer, and printer so you can print out sufficiently witchy-looking photos on the spot. Have index cards ready to paste the photos on, including such pertinent information as name, coven, and expiration date (April 30, of course!). Rubber-stamp the license with a witch on a broomstick, a raven, or another fitting image. If you don't have a laminating machine (who does?), you can cover the cards with clear packing tape to make them look official.

Seven
A Walpurgis Herbal

It is impossible to imagine Walpurgis Night without a fragrant veil of smoke hanging over the proceedings. Rosemary and juniper smoulder atop waving torches while thick clouds of steam laced with fennel and bear's garlic roll from the cauldron. Cold May punch flavored with sweet woodruff is passed from hand to hand to warm the heart, and green spring soup is drunk to cleanse the blood.

This chapter contains brief biographical sketches of thirteen herbs, each of which have something to do with witches, Walpurgis Night, and the sacred rites of spring. But they are by no means the only ones.

Other herbs known to make cameo appearances on May Eve include vervain, a plant so holy the Druids were moved to compensate the earth with a gift of honey when they plucked it;[1] mugwort, declared by the Anglo-Saxons as the mother of all herbs;[2] and thyme, with its power to smoke out witches, prevent nightmares,[3] and produce visions of fairies.[4]

A powder of dried cowslips gathered on Walpurgis Night was fed to German livestock to free them from enchantment.[5] Marjoram and gillyflowers were hung over the cattle stalls on that fateful eve, while a concoction of marjoram and valerian allowed one to witness the witches' flight to the Brocken without suffering harm.[6] A bunch of valerian, or chamomile, hung upside down, would betray a witch's presence by swinging in place.[7]

Bear's garlic, as we shall see, played a prominent role in the days leading up to April 30, but ordinary garlic, too, deserves mention: a garlic bulb was often placed at a crossroads, preferably at midnight, as an offering to Hecate, Greek goddess of witchcraft.[8]

And at midnight on Walpurgis Night, so it was said, the water in all the forest streams was magically turned to wine, but you would not be able to draw it into your cup unless you had a bit of fernseed about you.[9]

As if they did not have enough to do on their big night, witches were also believed to snip the leaves of the meadow saffron (*Colchicum autumnale*) and toss them into a poisonous salad. This is why the meadow saffron's leaves are often brown and shriveled at the tips, as if the plant itself had withered at the witches' touch.

Most of the herbs discussed in this chapter were used in, and as a protection against, witchcraft. Except for angelica, all of the herbs that have been used to divert enchantment were at the same time, supposedly, part of the witches' own potions. How did this come about? No doubt, certain herbs had long been regarded as magical because of the essential oils, vitamins, and minerals they contained. Some, like

valerian and wormwood, may have seeded the dreams of shamans. When those skilled in the use of these so-called magical herbs were vilified by the church, so was their pharmacopeia. Yet there persisted a parallel folk memory of these plants as a means of protection and healing.

Several of the herbs in this chapter, such as flax, angelica, and sweet woodruff, predate the written record north of the Rhine, while some of our most familiar cooking herbs found their first northern purchase in monastery gardens. Sage, rosemary, and garlic might never have found places at our table had not such luminaries as Charlemagne and Hildegard of Bingen been there to cheer them on. In the past, herbs were employed by everyone for just about everything. Nor did the need for herbs end with death; thyme, rosemary, and marjoram were thrown in after the casket, and the wealthy often willed money to the church for the strewing of expensive herbs on holy days.[10]

It is surprising to see how far some of our once-revered herbs have fallen. In the ninth century, the Anglo-Saxons still recognized the waybread, or plantain (*Plantago major*), as an herb sacred to the god Wodan. You may not recognize the waybread's name, but you've probably seen it a thousand times, its nubbly green-and-brown candles rising proudly from the sun-baked earth of a vacant lot or forcing their way through a crack in the sidewalk. Today we call it a weed, but its name in Old High German meant something like "King of the Road."[11]

Never heard of ground ivy (*Glechoma hederacea*)? Thick-stalked, with small violet flowers and evergreen leaves shaped like scalloped kidneys, this mint family

member also goes by the names *gill-on-the-ground*, *robin-runaway*, *alehoof*, and *crow victuals*.[12] You may not have heard any of those names either, but chances are you've seen it, for all ground ivy needs in order to thrive is shade, damp, and a little bit of neglect. When gathered on Walpurgis Night, a wreath of this unassuming ivy acts as a magic mirror, revealing both the presence of witches and their dark doings.[13]

Angelica (*Angelica archangelica*)

To speak the Latin name of this herb is to cue a heavenly choir. Here is a plant with a spotless reputation, one of the few—perhaps the only—that has never been listed as an ingredient in a witch's potion.[14] Its German name, *Brustwurz*, translates as "breast spice," and when worn close to the breast, there is no better protection against witchcraft,[15] plague, and evil in general.[16]

Angelica was as much revered by the pagans as it was by the monks who later invited it into their gardens. A northern native, angelica opens its foamy white umbrellas in mountainous regions and cool wet meadows all the way to Lapland. A candied angelica stalk was a gift fit for a queen: King Olav presents one to Queen Tyri in Snorri Sturluson's *Lives of the Norse Kings*.[17]

The hollow stalks, which can reach a height of six feet, are still candied and used to decorate fancy cakes in Europe. Though angelica was unknown to the Greeks and Romans, some of the best candied angelica now comes from Naples, Italy. The leaves and roots—and seeds, too—were used in

medieval cookery,[18] lending the food a taste similar to that of anise.

Anise (*Pimpinella anisum*)

So, you've invited a couple of hags over for tea and you don't know what to serve them. Aniseed is a good bet, especially if one of those hags is Black Annis, a horrible, blue-faced old giantess who liked to eat people and cattle but could be appeased with a dead cat marinated in anisette. Such an offering was made to her every Easter Monday in Leicestershire well into the Age of Reason. The association of aniseed with Black Annis probably came late in her career, for she is, in fact, one of the more frightening incarnations of the Celtic goddess Anu.[19]

Returning to the world of herbs, anise is the mighty angelica's sparser, more spidery southern cousin. What we call *aniseed* is actually the fruit of the plant.[20] Unlike angelica, anise does not do well in the cold and the wet but prefers a more Mediterranean environment.[21]

Today, aniseed is used to flavor breads and cookies like the molded German *Springerle.* Aniseed serves as a milk stimulant for nursing mothers, and in India is chewed as an after-dinner breath freshener.[22] King Edward IV of England scented his bed linens with sachets of aniseed.[23]

Bear's Garlic (*Allium ursinum*)

It is not quite clear how the bear's garlic got its name, but it may have something to do with the bear's standing in ancient Germanic religion.[24] The bear is the most ancient

of northern European cult animals, linking prehistoric Germanic tradition with the shamanism of Siberia. Apparently fearless, the bear was especially revered by warriors. The Norse sagas feature human characters who could turn themselves into bears,[25] while the bear could transform itself into a wild plant. The bear's garlic, then, is the vegetal manifestation of the bear's magic.[26] Why this shapeshifting king of the forest should have chosen *Allium ursinum* is a secret that probably died with the berserkers, or "bear shirts."[27]

Bear's garlic is actually more closely related to chives than to ordinary garlic, but its bulbs can be prepared just like the paper-skinned cloves you get in the grocery store. Outside the kitchen, bear's garlic, also known as *wild garlic* and *devil's posy*, is one of the best defenses against witchcraft, whether it is eaten, rubbed over the breast, or fed to cattle.[28]

But there's a twist! The witches were every bit as fond of bear's garlic as the common folk. Therefore, it had to be cleared from the forest floor before the witches swept through on their broomsticks on Walpurgis Night. Otherwise, the witches would pick it for their own evil potions.[29] In Thuringia, this frenzied harvest still takes place on the last weekend in April at the *Ramschelfest*—*Ramschel* being an old folk name for bear's garlic.[30] Originally, the plant was probably gathered by healers and shamans who knew of its blood-cleansing properties.[31]

There is one more reason for gathering bear's garlic before the end of April: in May, another plant with broad, dark green leaves makes its appearance on the forest floor.

It is the highly poisonous lily-of-the-valley—not a plant you want to end up on your Walpurgis table!

Chervil (*Anthriscus cerefolium*)

According to a little ditty in the tenth-century Anglo-Saxon manuscript *Lacnunga*, chervil was one of the nine herbs sacred to the god Wodan. (The other eight are mugwort, waybread, watercress, nettle, chamomile, fennel, crab-apple, and the mysterious "atterlothe."[32]) Chervil, like parsley, is a safe stand-in for hemlock, a plant it strongly resembles.[33] It also looks a lot like wild meadow chervil that can cause a nasty skin rash,[34] so if you don't want to get kicked out of your coven, you'd better get this one at the greenhouse instead of gathering it yourself.

While chervil repels snails and other pests in the garden, it does its best work in the kitchen. High in Vitamin C, it has long been a key ingredient in the green soups and sauces served in Germany in early spring.[35] A native of the Middle East, chervil was already known to the Anglo-Saxons of the tenth century. It became popular in medieval Europe as a blood cleanser after the long dark days of winter and also to keep people going during the privations of Lent.[36]

Dill (*Anethum graveolens*)

If you are an herb, *graveolens* at the end of your Latin name means you smell bad.[37] Dill's common name is a little more flattering: it comes from the Old English *dylle*, meaning "to soothe," probably because the seeds were made into a cordial to soothe gassy babies.[38]

Hang a bunch of dill in your doorway, and witches will not come into your house. Much though the witches were supposed to hate it, they used dill in their own potions[39] and it was a key ingredient in love philtres.[40] A native of southeastern Europe, it did not take long for dill to gain a foothold in northern kitchen gardens, probably because it is such a versatile pot herb. Neither pickles nor the Swedish salmon dish *gravlax* would be the same without it.

Fennel (*Foeniculum vulgare*)

Looks like celery, tastes like licorice:[41] not a bad combination. Like its distant carrot family cousin, dill, fennel was also used to quiet colicky babies and to ward off witches.[42] In ancient Greece, fennel seedlings were carried through the streets in pots to welcome spring.[43] In medieval Europe, it was used as a strewing herb, vegetable, gin flavoring,[44] aphrodisiac, and cure-all, supposedly effective against both snake venom and deadly mushrooms.[45]

Fennel's size also makes it a good hiding place. The Greek god Prometheus secreted fire in a fennel stalk in order to smuggle it down from Mount Olympus, and the pith, or heart of the stalk, can in fact be used as tinder. Ancient manuscripts, too, were rolled tight and hidden in fennel stalks.[46]

Flax (*Linum usitatissimum*)

The seeds of this plant are known as *flaxseed* when eaten and *linseed* when pressed for oil. Like angelica, flax has long been at home in the north. The Swiss lake-dwellers of the

second millennium BCE grew it for both food and clothing,[47] and it was used to make cordage for many thousands of years before that.[48]

The bast of the flax's inner bark is the source of linen. We have flax to thank for the term *white sale*, since linen thread is much more difficult to dye than its Indian successor, cotton. Between green plant and bedsheet stands a lot of hard work, including retting, braking, scutching, spinning, and weaving. Such an arduous process required a strong patroness, and the medieval housewife had one in Bertha/Holda.

The Bohemians believed that for six days of the week the flax was the province of Holda, but on Saturday it fell under the Devil's influence. One should, therefore, have nothing to do with the plant on Saturdays. Bavarian babies were placed amid the flax when ill and sprinkled with the seeds. Elsewhere in Germany, giddiness could be relieved by running three times naked around a plot of flax, and a pillow stuffed with flaxseed could cure a toothache. Bohemian maidens danced in the flax on their seventeenth birthdays, unless, of course, their birthdays fell on Saturdays.[49]

Witches supposedly abhorred the sky-blue flax flowers. For this reason, cattle were festooned with them and a pot of flax flowers was kept by the front door.[50] (If you want to keep flax blooming on your own doorstep, keep pinching back the faded blossoms so that new ones will grow.) The Abbess Walburga very likely kept a patch of flax at Heidenheim but for a very different reason: to provide linen for her own and the other nuns' wimples.[51] Charlemagne gave allowances for the

growing of flax for linen[52] and commanded his subjects to eat the seeds for the betterment of their health.[53]

Witches might not have liked the look of the flowers, but they had nothing against the seeds, which they gathered at the dark of the moon to add to their potions. A farmer could buy himself a whole trouble-free year just by giving a witch a handful of flaxseed.[54]

Juniper (Juniperus communis)

Juniper is one of the stars of Walpurgis Night. An evergreen, it was burned both to hallow and to disinfect the home at the end of the long winter. This herb is so powerful that you don't even have to burn it to keep evil spirits at bay—just place a sprig above the door.[55] An evergreen shrub that thrives on the heath, its berries are added to meat dishes and to sauerkraut.[56] The juniper gives its name to gin, via the French *genièvre*, "juniper."

A spirit resides in the juniper tree itself. Addressed as Frau Wacholder, or "Mrs. Juniper," she can be petitioned to retrieve stolen articles and bring the thieves to justice.[57]

"The Juniper Tree" is one of those Grimms' fairy-tales that seldom make it into modern anthologies. In the "Singing Bone" tradition of folktales, it recounts the fate of a little boy who is killed by his stepmother, baked into a pie, and fed to his unwitting father. The boy's sister has the presence of mind to deposit his bones inside a juniper tree (though, oddly enough, not to tell her father what has happened). The bones are transformed into a lovely singing bird who flies around the village singing out its story to everyone it meets. The bird receives gifts, one of which is a

millstone that it drops on the stepmother's head. At that, the boy is miraculously restored to his original form and reunited with his father and sister.[58] In some versions, the juniper is replaced by an almond tree, and the boy takes on aspects of Snow White. Since the juniper is native to Germany, while the almond is a more recent immigrant from the south, the juniper almost certainly represents the older tradition.

In North America, the cedar waxwing can become drunk on the fermented berries of *Juniperus virginiana.* Perhaps our ancestors witnessed the juniper's power to loosen the tongues of humans and make them give up the truth. By extension, the tree itself came to stand for justice, protection, and revenge.

It's best to stay away from juniper berries if you're pregnant. Their use as an abortifacient earned the juniper the nickname "bastard killer" in medieval England.

Mullein (*Verbascum thapsus*)

It is not clear whether the mullein got its nickname, "hag taper," because hags (i.e., witches) disliked it or because they carried the giant flower spikes themselves to light their way to their midnight revels.[59] The Romans certainly used it in their own ceremonies: the Latin *candelaria* refers to a spike of mullein that has been dried and dipped in tallow in order to be used as a torch.[60] Roman women mixed an infusion of the mullein's yellow flowers with lye to make a blond hair dye.[61] Earlier, the god Hermes gave Odysseus a spike of mullein to protect him from the witch Circe's

machinations. Today, mullein is the centerpiece of the giant herbal bouquets gathered in Germany in August.[62]

If you find the term *hag taper* offensive, the plant has plenty of other nicknames to choose from: *ice leaf, hare's beard, Our Lady's flannel, candlewick plant,*[63] *Jupiter's staff,* and *Aaron's rod,*[64] to name a few. You don't have to stray far from the roadside to find mullein. In North America, the great mullein grows to eight feet in height.[65] With its slender tower of yellow flowers, it's easy to spot and already looks like a candle. Mullein dies down to the ground in winter, but any break in the weather is enough to start it growing again.

Rosemary (*Rosmarinus officinalis*)

This herb's Latin name, *Rosmarinus*, means "dew of the sea," for the sprays of tiny bluish flowers grow wild all along the shores of the Mediterranean.[66] Christians later associated the name with the Virgin Mary.[67] Meanwhile, one of its Dutch names means "elf leaf," for the shrub was said to be haunted by the little people.[68]

Rosemary does not grow easily in northern climes, but the plant was so useful that it soon caught on, thanks to the combined efforts of Charlemagne, homeward-bound crusaders, and the great medieval trading companies.[69] Though expensive, rosemary was in great demand throughout the Middle Ages as a strewing herb, moth repellent,[70] fumigant (due to its high camphor content),[71] and pot herb.[72] It has been said that lavender smells sweeter, but the all-purpose rosemary was the preferred herb in medieval households.[73]

Like its fellow labiate, marjoram, rosemary was a frequent guest at both weddings and funerals. The plant's fragrance masked the smell of death, while German brides carried it to guard against pregnancy and an early end to the honeymoon.[74] Anne of Cleves wore rosemary in her coronet when she arrived in England to wed Henry VIII.[75] Perhaps the rosemary gave her good luck, for, unlike her successor Anne Boleyn, Anne of Cleves was divorced and allowed to die a natural death.

On the night of April 30, witch-fearing farmers of the Harz burned rosemary, juniper, and hemlock on their torches.[76] But rosemary was also essential to the fashionable witch's Walpurgis Night toilette: it was a key ingredient of Hungary water, Europe's first perfume.

Rue (*Ruta graveolens*)

There's that *graveolens* again. Witches, it has been said, dislike the smell of rue,[77] as do plague-bearing rats.[78] Rue is and always has been an herb with an identity disorder. A common ingredient in witches' potions, it was also at the forefront in the battle against said witches.[79] Rue—along with rosemary, juniper, blackthorn, wild caper, and hemlock—was traditionally gathered on a Thursday and burnt on Walpurgis Night by laymen specially blessed by the church for this task. Certainly, the smoke of these burning herbs got rid of the bugs that had taken up residence during the winter,[80] but the witches likely remained unfazed. "By yarrow and rue and my red cap, too," cried the witches of Irish legend before mounting their broomsticks and rising up the chimney.[81]

Confusion prevails even in the herb's names. Colloquially known as *herb-of-grace*,[82] *rue* means quite the opposite, coming from the Old English *hreowan*, meaning "to distress."[83] Speakers of Old English employed rue against the effects of monkshood, mistletoe, and salamander bites,[84] as well as all manner of diseases and plain old evil in general.[85] Churchmen used it for sprinkling holy water, especially during exorcisms,[86] while the layman used it to control unwelcome infestations of pixies, elves, brownies, and the like.[87]

Rue's powerful scent rules it out as a kitchen herb. But do plant one in your garden and see what happens. Sooner or later, the neighborhood witch will stop by and ask to borrow some. Or, more probably, she will steal it, for rue, like many herbs, grows best when it is taken without asking.[88]

Here is an American footnote to the story of witches and rue: an English gentleman traveling through the colonies in the late seventeenth century observed that hardly any "rewe" grew in the vicinity of Salem, Massachusetts.[89]

Sage (*Salvia officinalis*)

"He who would live for aye, must eat sage in May,"[90] goes the ancient saying, which must have actually rhymed in olden days. You may be familiar with "sage" as a Native American smudging herb. Is this the same sage to which medieval Europeans attached their magical beliefs? The answer to this question would have to be both yes and no. Several of the herbs we have dubbed "sage" in North America are in fact related to *Salvia officinalis*. Sagebrush, however, is an artemisia and therefore more closely related to mugwort than to Old World sage.[91]

Like its boon companions rosemary and thyme, sage is an evergreen shrub that first grew around the Mediterranean. Its spikes of purple-blue flowers summon butterflies and bees,[92] while the fragrant oils coursing through its leaves repel pests both natural and supernatural. At the onset of spring, sage was burnt to purify the house and drunk in a tonic to cleanse the blood. The medievals also believed it could make one wise, or "sage."

Sweet Woodruff (*Galium odoratum*)

If you have room for only one herb in your Walpurgis Night celebration, make it this one. You can find seedlings at just about any garden center, and it isn't particular about where it grows. Now a common border plant, sweet woodruff's first home was the deep, dark Eurasian forest.[93] Known to the Saxons as *wuderofe*,[94] this humble-looking creeper had a sure place in the hearts of the common people long before Charlemagne enforced the growing of herbs among his subjects. To this day, sweet woodruff is an essential ingredient of the German *Maibowle*, or cold May punch.[95]

The "sweet" part of the plant's name refers to its fragrance, which is strongest after drying[96] and when crushed underfoot, endearing it to generations of medieval housewives.[97] *Wood*, obviously, refers to its sylvan habitat, while *ruff*, *rofe*, or *rove* is such an old word that its meaning has been lost. The German name *Waldmeister* means "master of the forest."

Sweet woodruff should be harvested before May, when it puts out tiny white flowers. Throw a bunch of it in your

punch bowl or scatter it around your dancing ground, to release its sweet, wild scent into the night.

RECIPE: COLD MAY PUNCH

Like fire, May wine is central to the celebration of Walpurgis Night and has been for at least a thousand years. There are as many recipes for Maibowle, or cold May punch, as there have been generations drinking it. The one thing the recipes all have in common is white wine and the essence of sweet woodruff. The scent of this herb when dried has been likened to freshly mown hay. To me, it smells like the darkest part of the forest: deep, green, and wild.

Ingredients:

- 7 short sprigs sweet woodruff, picked before blooming and hung up to dry for 2–3 days (you can get sweet woodruff at just about any garden center)
- 2 cups inexpensive white wine (for a nonalcoholic version, just increase the seltzer and grape juice)
- 1 cup seltzer
- 1 cup white grape juice
- 4 tablespoons vanilla sugar (this is white sugar in which a vanilla bean has been hanging out for at least a few days; one vanilla bean can last for years—just keep topping off the sugar, and keep it in an airtight container)
- strawberries
- mineral water (optional)

Put the dried sweet woodruff in the wine and leave it for at least two hours in the refrigerator. Then strain out the herb and discard it.

Pour the wine, seltzer, and white grape juice into a punch bowl. Add the vanilla sugar and watch it fizz.

If you have small, fresh strawberries, add them fresh to the punch. Or, you can cut larger strawberries in quarters and freeze them with water in ice cube trays. Add to the punch at the last minute. If you're worried about the ice cubes melting over the course of the evening and "flattening" the punch, use mineral water instead of tap.

RECIPE: FENNEL, CHICKEN, AND POTATO SOUP

Ingredients:

1½ tablespoons butter
6 small yellow potatoes
½ bulb fennel
1 chicken breast, sliced thin
1½ cups chicken stock
1½ cups water
salt to taste

Remove both the stalks and the tough base or pith from the fennel bulb but set aside the feathery green leaves for garnish. (And for your crappy-weather tea—see the recipe for same in this chapter!) Slice the bulb as you would an onion. Melt the butter in a soup pot, then add the fennel, potatoes, and a pinch of salt. Sauté for about three minutes. Add the chicken stock and simmer covered for five minutes or until the fennel softens and the potatoes are almost done.

Add the water, return the soup to a boil, then add the chicken slices one at a time. Cook for five more minutes or until chicken is cooked through.

Garnish with fennel leaves and serve.

RECIPE: GREEN SOUP

The typical German spring soup is usually a cream soup. You can make spring soup by substituting chervil for the feature ingredient in any cream soup recipe, so long as you remember not to add it until the very last minute. You can freeze chervil, but overcooking it causes it to lose a lot of its character. Since my family is not wild about cream soups, I feed them this alternative.

Ingredients:

1 tablespoon butter or olive oil
1 tablespoon diced pancetta (optional)
½ small yellow onion, chopped
1 small yellow potato, peeled and cut up
about 12 ounces or one bunch asparagus (frozen will do)
2 cups chicken stock
2 cups water
1 scant cup fresh or frozen chervil, chopped

Melt the butter in a heavy sauce pan. Add the pancetta and onion and sauté until the onion is glassy. Stir in the potatoes, then the asparagus. Add the chicken stock and water, bring to a boil, and simmer until the potatoes and asparagus are tender. Remove from heat, add chervil, and blend to a smooth green—bits of chervil leaves should still be visible.

Season with salt and pepper and serve.

RECIPE: CRAPPY-WEATHER TEA

"Crappy-weather tea" is a polite translation of the Low German *Schietwettertee*. Brewing this tea will neither cause nor

prevent crappy weather, but it will make you feel cosy inside even in the heaviest of spring rains. Since the weather is often stormy on the Brocken, bring a thermos of this tea if you are going that way.

Ingredients:

- leaves of 16 strawberries
- leaves of 1 fennel bulb
- ½ Golden Delicious apple, peeled and cut into thin wedges
- 1 teaspoon aniseed
- 1 teaspoon dried elderberries or contents of 1 elderberry tea bag
- 1 teaspoon dried rosehips or contents of 1 rosehip tea bag
- (You can find plain elderberry and rosehip teas in a health-food or organic grocery store.)

Wash the strawberry and fennel leaves, then spread them out on a paper towel in a warm, dry place for 2–3 days.

Spread the apple wedges on a foil or parchment-lined baking sheet and bake at 300°F for 45 minutes. When cool, break them into bits and leave them to dry a few more hours.

Combine all ingredients in an airtight tin for a few days to let the flavors meld. When ready to brew, steep the tea for at least six minutes, using a tea ball or fine sieve.

Makes two pots, or about six cups, of tea.

CRAFT: WALPURGIS WAND

This is a smudge wand or smudge "stick," as it is also called. To "smudge" is to create a protective veil of smoke for the

purpose of driving away illness, insects, frost, and all manner of bad influences. In the Old World, it is *Juniperus communis* that is used for purification. In the New World, *Juniperus monosperma* and *Juniperus virginiana* are the herbs of choice. I have used *Juniperus virginiana,* or eastern red cedar, since that's what grows near my home. It pays to honor the local tree spirits, so use whichever member of the *Juniperus* family grows near you.

Likewise, the sage used here is the Mediterranean *Salvia officinalis*, or "true" sage, because that's what I found in the grocery store. (I'm more of a gatherer than a grower.) If you live out west, you probably don't have to go far to find one of the equally sacred and smudgeable *Artemisias*, so go ahead and gather those instead. Whichever herbs you use, gather only what you need, don't pull up anything by the roots, and never take the last one.

You will need:

- 1 bunch fresh juniper/cedar cuttings (leave on any of the beautiful, dusty blue berries that come with it)
- 1 bunch fresh sage
- 1 bunch fresh rosemary
- 2 lengths perle cotton, about 7 feet each, in contrasting colors (plain cotton string will also do)
- scissors
- rubber bands

Line up your juniper sprigs and trim off the needles from the last inch or so of the twig ends. Now, gather them into a bundle, making sure the twig ends are even. Secure them tightly with a rubber band. (You'll remove it later.)

Now add the rosemary and sage to the outside of the bundle, keeping the stalks and leaves parallel with the juniper twigs as best you can. Holding the whole bouquet firmly in hand, snip off and remove the first rubber band, replacing with another further up so that sage, rosemary, and juniper are all held firmly together.

Lay the bundle on the table in front of you. Using the two strings as one, secure a loop at the base of the wand, as in the witch's broom craft (chapter 6). When you have woven the strings around the base of the wand, work your way up, winding the strings, still together, around the bundle like the stripes on a candy cane. When you reach the top, you can start back down, again candy-cane fashion, crisscrossing your earlier effort. Wind the strings a few more times tightly around the base, insert the ends through the loop and pull tightly to secure.

Tie the two different colored ends together to make a loop by which to hang your wand. You can either trim off the ragged top or leave it looking wild. If you're not happy with your smudge wand, if you think it looks too fat and untidy, don't throw it away! Remove the strings after a day or two and try again. The herbs will already be molded into shape and will be easier to handle this time. If you find that the juniper is just too unruly, take off all the needles and use bare juniper twigs to form the core of your wand. (You can add the needles to all the other fallen bits, placing them in a bowl or pouch to make Walpurgis potpourri. When it's dry, you can drop pinches of the herbs into a hot frying pan to make smoke.)

When you're finally happy with your wand, hang it upside down in a dry place where your friends can admire your

handiwork. In a few weeks, it will be ready to use for smudging. Light the tip of the wand only, then blow out the flame. A fine, fragrant thread of smoke should rise from the bundle. Carry it from room to room, waving to disperse the smoke to all corners, or leave it propped up on a plate in the center of your home. If the wand is still smoking when you're ready to put it away, you will have to stub it out or, in extreme cases, dowse it in water. Don't worry; it will dry out again.

Unless you're especially smudge-happy, a single, dense smudge wand should last you about a year.

CRAFT: HERB BELLS

In the old days, herb seedlings were sheltered under graceful, bell-shaped glasses. If you can't afford an antique bell glass, trying making one of these.

For each bell you will need:

1 liter-size seltzer or other clear plastic bottle
a 1¼" wooden bead or knob
white acrylic or craft paint
small paintbrush
water-insoluble glue
masking tape or rubber band
scissors

Put the masking tape or rubber band around the bottle about four inches from the neck. Use this as a guide to cut around. (To start cutting, you will have to use your scissors to stab the bottle further down, then cut your way up to the masking tape circle.)

Now that you've cut out your "bell," glue the wooden bead over the mouth of the bottle to create a handle or finial. Paint the neck and the bead white.

Place the bell over one of your herb seedlings in its pot to hold in moisture. You can also use herb bells outside to protect your baby herbs against late frosts.

For variety, make several bells using different brands of bottles—they will have slightly different shapes.

CRAFT: RUNIC GARDEN STAVES

You will need:

popsicle sticks
gold or silver permanent metallic markers

Using the Elder Futhark (see chapter 9) or runic alphabet of your choice, write the names of any herbs you are growing on the popsicle sticks, then stick them in the soil. They'll look intriguing there, as well as reinforce your knowledge of the runes every time you look at them.

"But I'm not sure how to spell *common toadflax* in runes!"

Don't worry! At the time the runes were in general use, there was no such thing as standardized spelling. Just do your best.

If you're not a gardener, you can identify and label the wild trees and plants growing around your home, creating your own runic arboretum without planting a seed!

CRAFT: HAG TAPER

You will need:

1 yellow taper candle
5 mullein leaves (or felt)
floral tape

The yellow taper will represent the mullein stalk with its yellow flowers. Use floral tape to bind five mullein leaves, overlapping, to the base of the candle. See Figure 1. (If you really can't find any mullein leaves, you can cut your own out of light green felt.) Fold the leaves back so they lie as they did on the plant. See Figure 2. This is a good candle to use in processions, since the leaves protect the hand from any dripping wax. You can also put them in candle holders on the table.

Figure 1

Figure 2

Eight
The Walpurgis Table

Wouldn't it be nice if everyone who reads this book could spend their next Walpurgis Night cavorting in the fog on top of the Brocken? That said, most of us will probably have to find a mountain, hill, hillock, or bump in the road closer to home. If you're a city dweller, you may have to center your festivities around the kitchen table.

Whatever your means, environment, or spatial challenges, this chapter is for you. The most important ingredient of a Walpurgis Night feast is imagination, so let's put off our supper-making for a moment and set off in search of ideas. We've been exploring the German celebration of *Walpurgisnacht*; now let's take a side trip to the other countries where the date of April 30 is circled in fire. We'll examine the customs, sample the fare, and hopefully take away with us the true essence of May Eve.

Why does Walpurgis Night persist in the festival calendars of some countries and not of others? Germany was the Abbess Walburga's adopted homeland and remains the epicenter of the Walpurgis tradition. One might expect this

tradition to be common to all German-speaking nations. Not so.

Walburga's cloister was actually closer to the present-day Swiss and Austrian borders than it was to the Brocken, yet today April 30 goes mostly unnoticed in Switzerland and Austria. As a matter of fact, the residents of those countries start to drive winter out in January already with the *Perchtenlauf*, a very Walpurgis-like confusion of bells, whips, and frightening costumes. And besides, one can hardly expect the witches of the Alps to depart their eyries for a mere 3,747-foot molehill like the Brocken!

Norwegian witches, too, had mountains of their own and were farther removed from Central European tradition than their Swedish neighbors. The Finns are even more distant, both geographically and linguistically, but their observance of Walpurgis Night is much younger and less mystical than we see in Germany and the Czech Republic. Moravian witches repaired to Mt. Radost, while Danish witches took themselves all the way to Mt. Hekla in Iceland rather than cross the oft-contested German border.

If there was in fact a goddess Walpurga, her cult most likely evolved somewhere in the Lowlands. Yet none of today's Lowland countries, nor even Denmark or extreme northern Germany, celebrate her namesake's feast day. This may be due to the clean sweep of Protestantism or the influence of those early English missionaries.

Walpurgis Night is not unknown in France, where they still have a thriving May Day celebration. But *La Nuit de Walpurgis* is not nearly as much of a to-do as *Walpurgisnacht*. This difference reminds us of the bloody line that

was drawn between Christian Franks and pagan Saxons in Charlemagne's time. In general, Walpurgis Night survives in those regions that were for much of their histories both beyond the pale of Western Christendom and just out of reach of Christian Byzantium.

Valborg

In Sweden, April 30 is known as *Valborgsmässoafton*, or *Valborg* for short. Bonfires blaze, especially in the east of Sweden, but they have little to do with witches anymore. Reserving the broomsticks and kerchiefs for Easter, on Valborg Swedish students and former students don white caps, symbols of scholarship, and greet the spring with old-fashioned songs. Scandinavia at this time of year is not yet quite warm, so the bonfires round which they belt out their tunes serve as a promise of the summertime to come. The fires are built of junk and worn-out household items, a dramatic climax to spring cleaning.

Dinner on Valborgsmässoafton usually features *gravlax*—thin slices of salmon that have been marinated, not cooked, in salt, sugar, and dill. I'm sure the Swedes know exactly what they're doing, but if you, like me, are a little leery of serving up raw salmon that's been sitting in the refrigerator for three days, here's an alternative:

RECIPE: SMOKED SALMON WITH MUSTARD DILL SAUCE

1 package smoked salmon
about 2 tablespoons Dijon mustard
about 2 tablespoons honey

about 2 tablespoons chopped fresh dill
Swedish crisp bread or baby potatoes

What about all the *abouts*? The amounts depend on how sweet or spicy you want your sauce to be and how much you like the taste of fresh dill. You can start out with one tablespoon of each ingredient, then decide which flavor you want to bring out. When you've made the sauce the way you like it, spoon it over the salmon on open-face crisp-bread sandwiches, or serve salmon and sauce with boiled baby potatoes.

If you really don't like mustard, serve the smoked salmon with a dollop of sour cream and sprinkle with capers. Capers, like the ash buds of which the Oldenburg witches were so fond, are not berries but the pickled buds of the caperbush.

RECIPE: SWEDISH CRISP BREAD

Yes, you can buy crisp bread in a paper package at the grocery store, but this will look and taste much more like what the Vikings ate.

Ingredients:

For the cookie sheet:
butter for greasing
1 teaspoon fennel seeds

For the dough:
1 package active dry yeast
½ teaspoon sugar
⅔ cup milk
1 cup whole wheat flour

1 cup white flour
⅓ cup rolled oats
¼ cup sunflower seeds, chopped
1 teaspoon butter, softened

Grease a large cookie sheet with butter and sprinkle with fennel seeds.

Mix sugar and yeast together in a large bowl. Heat the milk in a pot until it's very warm, but not hot and definitely not boiling. Pour half of the warm milk into the yeast mixture and stir. Set aside for five minutes.

Add remaining ingredients to yeast/milk mixture and knead together with your fingers until it's as smooth as you can make it. Divide the dough into six parts, roll each part into a ball, and flatten between your palms. Place the rounds on the cookie sheet, pressing them into the fennel seeds. Cover with a slightly damp dish towel and let rest in a warm place about half an hour.

Transfer rounds to a lightly floured board and roll each one as flat as you can with a rolling pin or a juice glass turned on its side. Prick all over with a fork, pressing the tines all the way through the dough. Be creative and make a pattern, such as a whirling spiral, to symbolize the turning of the year.

As you return your rolled-out circles of dough to the cookie sheet, you may find they no longer fit. You can either grease and seed another cookie sheet or bake them in two batches.

Bake crisp breads at 350°F for 15 minutes or until golden on top. Present them in a basket beside a platter of smoked salmon with mustard dill sauce.

Vappu

In its current form, *Vappu*, the Finnish celebration of May Day/Eve, dates only to the 1700s, its signature ritual to 1932. This ritual is the "capping" of Havis Amanda, a nude statue that poses atop a fountain in Helsinki's market square. Other than a bit of bronze drapery clutched between her thighs, the white student's cap is the only garment she wears all year. No doubt Havis Amanda is as glad as the cavorting university students to know that spring is on its way.

Masks and brightly colored balloons contribute to Vappu's carnival-like atmosphere, as do the rivers of wine and *sima*, a kind of mead made from lemons and honey or sugar.

RECIPE: SIMA

This is a kind of mead, the drink of choice of the Vikings and other early Scandinavian peoples. Sima, the traditional Finnish May Day drink, is only mildly alcoholic; the longer you let it ferment, the less mildly alcoholic it will be. It's customarily served with *Tippaleivät*, or Finnish May Day fritters (see the next recipe).

Ingredients:

1 quart water
1 lemon, impeccably clean
¼ cup + 1 teaspoon sugar
¼ cup honey
⅛ teaspoon active dry yeast
5 raisins

You will also need:

2 wide-mouthed glass juice bottles, at least one liter each, also impeccably clean

sieve or cheesecloth

Put the water on to boil.

Using a potato peeler or cheese grater, scrape the zest from the lemon. (The zest is the outermost, yellowmost part of the peel. It will amount to no more than a tablespoon.) Put the zest into one of the empty juice bottles.

Cut your half-naked lemon into quarters and squeeze the juice into the same bottle. Don't worry if a few seeds slip in; you'll get them out later. Add the honey and the ¼ cup sugar.

When the water is boiling, add it to the bottle, not quite filling it. Let the mixture stand until it is no longer hot but still very warm. Add yeast, stir, and let stand for at least twelve hours, leaving the bottle open. It you're afraid something might fly in there, cover the mouth of the bottle with cloth.

The next day, put one teaspoon white sugar and the raisins in the second bottle. Strain the mixture from the first bottle and pour it into the second bottle. Cover loosely. Leave your sima at room temperature for one to three days. A little foam at the top is a sign that fermentation is taking place. The raisins are supposed to rise to the top to indicate when the mead is ready to chill and drink. If the room is very warm, however, the raisins may rise prematurely.

When you think your sima is sufficiently "sparkly," strain it once more and chill for several hours before serving.

RECIPE: FINNISH MAY DAY FRITTERS

Finnish May Day fritters are similar to Pennsylvania Dutch funnel cakes, though somewhat lighter. In Finland, they are called *Tippaleivät* or *Tippaleipä*, meaning "drop cake" or "drop bread."

Ingredients:

- 1 egg
- 1 tablespoon sugar
- ¾ cup milk
- 1¼ cups flour
- vegetable oil for frying
- confectioner's sugar

Whisk egg and sugar together in a bowl. Stir in milk and flour. Don't use a mixer; this could make the batter too tough. The batter will be somewhat stiffer than pancake batter.

Fill a frying pan with ¼ inch to ½ inch of oil and heat until the oil is hot enough to ripple slightly.

For the next step, you can use either a pastry bag or a strong zipper bag with one corner cut off. Keep the hole small. (The Finns have special funnels for pouring the batter in the pan, as well as Finnish grandmothers to show them how to use them.)

Fill the bag of your choice with batter. Hold it over the pan and squeeze the batter into the hot oil in a swirling motion. Unlike funnel cake, which fills the pan, Tippaleivät are about the size of doughnuts. A metal ring or round cookie cutter will help the pastry keep its shape. You don't have to use a ring, but be prepared for your Tippaleivät to come out

looking more like carpet beaters than the traditional bird's-nest shape.

Fry each pastry for about 15 seconds on each side or until they turn golden. If they're still yellow after 15 seconds, it means the oil is not hot enough.

Drain finished pastries on a paper towel, sprinkle with confectioner's sugar, and serve warm.

Čarodějnice and the Burning of Morena

Čarodějnice, or *Pálení Čarodějnic*—as Walpurgis Night in the Czech Republic is known—translates variously as "Day of the Witches," "Witches' Night," and, most appropriately, "Burning of the Witches." First and foremost, burning witches is what the festival is all about, though nowadays the witches are burned in effigy. Secondary to the celebration are beer drinking, sausage eating, and one-upmanship.

Although it looks a lot like the German Walpurgisnacht, Čarodějnice is recognized as the eve of St. Phillip's and St. Jacob's Day rather than St. Walburga's. Some believe it originated with the Iron Age Celts. The regions of Bohemia and Moravia were Celtic territory in those days,[1] and April 30, Beltane, was one of the Celts' four high holy days.

In neighboring Slovakia, it is winter that is put to death in the form of the Slavic goddess Morena.[2] Morena, or Morana, is the queen of winter and the dead. A straw figure dressed in peasant garb, Morena was carried in procession through the village to the riverbank. No easy death for this queen of the underworld: first she was stripped, her straw body set alight, then she was thrown into the icy water. This

custom is still observed in Slovakia, but not on April 30; the Burning of Morena takes place two weeks before Easter.

Once winter has been shown the door, it's time to let love in. As in Germany, Czech youths leave green branches on their sweethearts' doorsteps on May Eve. Leaping over the embers of the bonfire is a good way to show off for your beloved, but don't try this outside of the Czech Republic—or inside it, for that matter. The wee hours of May morning bring an increase in out-of-control fires and emergency-room visits, most of them for the treatment of burns.[3]

The Czech people take bonfire building very seriously indeed. In Sweden, the pyre might be just a haphazard pile of junk, but in the Czech Republic it is a work of art. There are three distinct types of bonfire: the teepee, the pagoda, and the "Burning Man," a form perfected over the last forty years by the town of Kozojedy. You can achieve the greatest height with the Burning Man (twenty meters, or about sixty-six feet),[4] while the villages of Řevnice and Mnichovice are in competition to see who can build the tallest pagoda. In 2004, the record specimen stood at fourteen meters, twenty centimeters.[5] For safety, bonfires are usually built close to the river, though safety seems to be a relative term on Witches' Night.

The witch herself is constructed much like our Halloween scarecrows: two sticks bound crosswise, dressed in old clothes, and stuffed with straw. She can also be made out of an old broom, and given a painted face, pointed hat, straw hair, and so on. At nightfall, she is paraded around and finally heaved up on top of the bonfire. In some regions, she is drowned as an added insult.

Of course, it doesn't take a fourteen-meter-high bonfire to burn a single effigy. Once the witch is dead, sausages are roasted in the flames. The sausages are accompanied by bread, mustard, beer, singing, and all-around carousing.

Within the city of Prague, the lighting of fires is strictly forbidden. So how do the city folk celebrate Čarodějnice? They light fires! It's a busy night for the fire department, but it's hard to curb an ancient tradition.

Safer celebrations take place on Petrin Hill and other green spaces within the city limits. On Kampa Island, separated from the rest of Prague by the "Devil's Stream," you can listen to music and buy a wide variety of witch-related trinkets. In Ladronka Park in 2008, another new record was set: a whopping 934 witches assembled there on April 30, almost a hundred more than the year before. What makes a witch a witch? Well, on Čarodějnice, all you need is a cape and a broomstick, both of which were distributed free of charge.[6] Children are intrinsic to the Czech celebration of May Eve. Not only do they dress up (a three-year-old girl won "Best Witch" at Kampa Island in 2006), they're actually helping to build the bonfires. There are occasional casualties; several years ago, fifteen children from the village of Nachod were hospitalized with burns.[7] Still, one can't help but wonder who has more fun: the American child who is forced to go trick-or-treating in the mall on Halloween or the little Czech villagers who have the honor of setting a twenty-foot-high pile of logs on fire on Witches' Night?

CRAFT: MAGIC RUNE LANTERN

For Čarodějnice 2007, the witches of Prague created a lovely spectacle as they proceeded through the streets with Chinese paper lanterns. This paper lantern will keep its secret until the flame is lit.

You will need:

- 2 sheets 8½" x 14" color copier paper, both of the same color (lighter colors work best)
- 1 round 11 cm cheese box—the kind that spreadable cheese wedges, such as The Laughing Cow®, come in
- glue
- small paper bathroom cup
- tea light
- scissors
- thin wire
- hole puncher
- fireplace match
- forked stick or dowel with a loop on one end

Glue the paper bathroom cup to the center of the bottom half of your cheese box. This is the base of your lantern. Place the tea light inside the cup and set aside.

Decide which runes you want to feature on your lantern. (See "Fun with Runes," chapter 9.) Cut straight, narrow strips from one of the sheets of paper. Use the strips to form the runes. Glue your runic sentiment down *backwards* on the second sheet of paper. (Second sheet should be sideways.)

When the glue is dry, roll the sheet loosely with the runes hidden inside the roll. Dab the outside bottom edge

with glue and place the roll inside the lantern base. Glue the vertical seam of the lantern closed.

Now, cut out the center of the cheese-box lid. Glue the rim of the lid to the top of your lantern. If you want to use it as a table lantern, you can light it now with the fireplace match and watch your runes magically appear. If you want to be able to carry your lantern, punch holes in the top rim and attach a wire handle. You can carry it by hooking the forked stick under the wire.

CRAFT: WITCH'S BREW POUCH

A "Witch's Brew" is an assortment of both smooth and cut Czech glass seed beads in colors ranging from black to gray in opaque, iridescent, and opalescent finishes. Nowadays, you can get decent seed beads made in Japan but the Czech kind are still the best! The beads are European, but for this craft we borrow our technique from the Woodlands tribes of North America. The pouch features a universally mystic spiral design.

You will need:

- scrap paper
- 1 piece light-colored chamois, buckskin, or felt about 6" long and 4" wide
- charcoal pencil
- dime or nickel (or another small coin)
- size 13 Witch's Brew mix of Czech glass seed beads (if you're a beginning beader, you might want to use a larger size, such as 12s or 11s)

beading thread and "sharps" or needles to go with your size beads (you can order these from your bead supplier)
glover's needle (your beading shop should have these, too)
sewing needle
sewing thread to match your material
waxed dental floss
scissors
utility knife
pinking shears
about 2½ feet satin or polyester ribbon, ⅛ inch wide

First, make a paper template in the shape you want your pouch to be. In the old days, small pouches were made from the beaded uppers of worn-out moccasins—i.e., straight sides, rounded bottoms, a little taller than wide. Place the template on your chamois and trace around it with the charcoal pencil. Cut out and repeat. Now you have a front and a back for your pouch. Straight edges are boring, so trim the tops with pinking shears. Set the back piece aside.

Place the dime on the soft side of the front piece and trace around it. (If you are using size 12 or larger beads, use a nickel.) Mark the exact center of the circle you have just traced. You will create your beaded spiral inside this circle.

Thread your beading needle or "sharp" with beading thread, and knot the end. Bring the needle and thread up through the mark in the center of the circle. If you are using buckskin, you may have to use the sewing needle to make the hole for the delicate sharp to pass through. In European beadwork, the sharp passes in and out of the fabric, picking

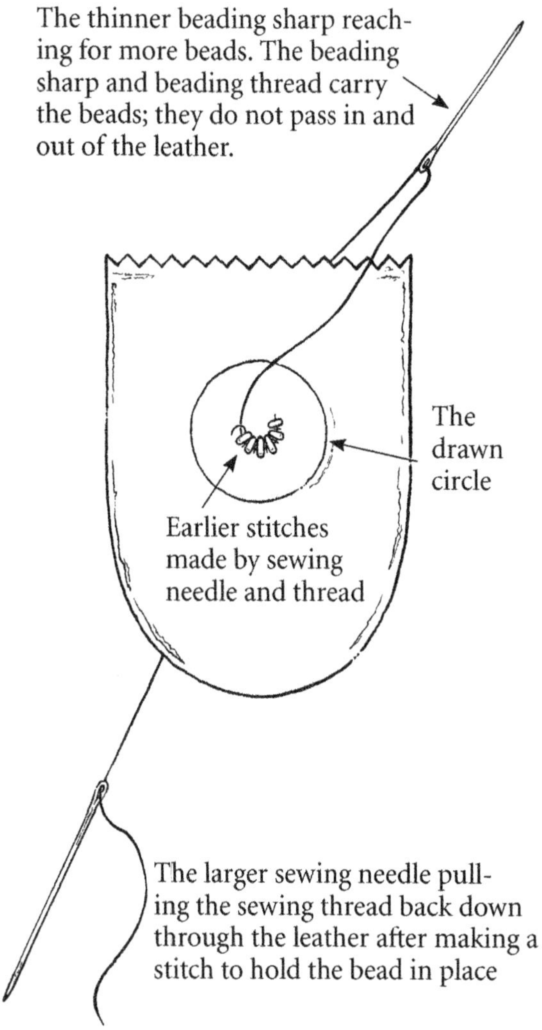
The thinner beading sharp reaching for more beads. The beading sharp and beading thread carry the beads; they do not pass in and out of the leather.
The drawn circle
Earlier stitches made by sewing needle and thread
The larger sewing needle pulling the sewing thread back down through the leather after making a stitch to hold the bead in place

Figure 1

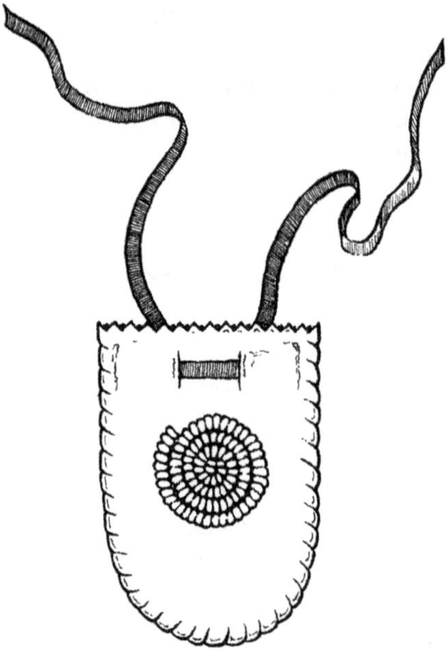

Figure 2

up beads one at a time. In much of Native American beadwork, as in this craft, the beading needle and thread pass through the leather only at the very beginning and end of the pattern. It is the larger sewing needle and sewing thread that pass in and out of the chamois, stitching the beading thread with its beads into place. See Figure 1.

How to transfer beads from the hank on which they are sold to the beading needle and thread: open up the plastic bag in which you bought your hank, separate one of the cotton strings, and poke your sharp into the first bead. Let it slide down the beading thread to rest on the chamois. (It is easiest to work by picking up only one or two beads at a time, but if it helps you to visualize the project, pick up a

large number of beads now, and coil them up in a spiral inside the charcoal circle. Now all you have to do is stitch the spiral into place with the sewing needle and thread.)

Bring the sewing needle and thread up through the chamois very close to the first bead and make a small, neat stitch over the beading thread. Continue to pick up beads and stitch them into place. Since the curve of the spiral is very tight at this point, you will need to stitch the beads down one at a time. As you work your way outward, you can stitch them down two and three at a time. When your spiral fills the circle, pass both sewing needle and sharp to the backside of the chamois and knot off the threads.

Use waxed dental floss to whip stitch the front and back of the pouch together. If you are using buckskin, you will need a glover's needle to pass through the double thickness of the leather. With the utility knife, cut four slits toward the top of the pouch, two in front and two in back, to pass the ribbon through. See Figure 2.

Fill your pouch with Walpurgis potpourri (see Walpurgis wand craft in chapter 7) and wear around your neck.

CRAFT: SHIP OF THE VANIR SALT CELLAR

From the Bronze Age down to the Viking Age, one of the most popular artistic motifs in the Baltic Sea area was, not surprisingly, the ship. It was etched into swordblades, cast on coins, and carved on the faces of monumental stones.[8] The ship was everywhere, but its most profound expression was the funerary ship.

The first "ship settings" or boat-shaped graves are clues to a spiritual transformation that was taking place in Europe

during the second century BCE.[9] These burials did not actually contain ships; rather, the ship-shaped grave mound was enclosed by stones cut and arranged so that the whole thing resembled one of the shallow, wide-bellied vessels of the time.[10] These "ships" were pure symbol, intended to bear the occupant not to another earthly realm but to an abstract afterlife. This tradition would eventually extend all the way from Estonia in the east to Sutton Hoo, in Britain, in the west.

By the much later Migration Period, actual boats were going into the ground with the deceased. While it's disappointing on the one hand to watch the cult becoming so literal-minded, we can only be thankful for such burials, for they've left us with the best-preserved examples of pre-Viking and Viking ships.

Ship burials were not for everyone, but the practice did cross a lot of the usual boundaries. Funeral ships hold the remains of both men and women, the rich and the not-so-rich, the interred and the cremated. The connecting thread may have been devotion to the Vanir, the Germanic—and possibly pre-Germanic—fertility gods. The noble Oseberg lady, who died in 834 AD and whose ship was so beautifully preserved in its tomb of blue clay in southern Norway, also had a wagon and four sledges with her. It is tempting to imagine that she might have been a priestess and was expected to use these conveyances to continue her ritual processions into the afterlife.[11]

The Bronze Age appearance of the boat-shaped grave may have marked the birth of the cult of the Vanir. The god Frey and the goddess Freya were the children of Njord, god

of the sea, and Njord's own sister. It is not certain whether this sister was the giantess Skadi, who lived in the mountains, or the island-dwelling Nerthus,[12] who used to travel round and bless the fields. Whichever she was, her children represent the fruitfulness that results from the meeting of earth and water.

Frey and Freya, Vanir par excellence, encompass the entire cycle of human life, from first love to final curtain. Freya is both goddess of love and chooser of the slain. Frey is the harvest god, but he is not bound to the earth; the dwarfs made him a ship of his own: *Skidbladnir*, meaning "skate blade." Within it, Frey could fit the entire company of the gods. When it is not needed, it can be folded up and put in a pouch![13]

In folklore, salt represents purity and offers protection from evil. In Germany, witches were believed to gather at salt springs and salt pans, suggesting that the boiling down of salt was once a duty performed by priestesses. Rather than put an ordinary salt shaker on your Walpurgis table, make your own ship-shaped salt cellar out of aluminum foil.

You will need:

1 sheet aluminum foil, about 2 feet long
banana
sea salt

Place the banana lengthwise in the center of the sheet of foil, bringing the edges of the foil up (shiny side out) and molding around the banana to form a long, curved Viking boat shape. Remove the banana. Twist the ends of the foil

Figure 1

to make narrow rods, then curl them over into spirals to resemble the curving stems of the Oseberg ship. See Figure 1.

Fill your ship with sea salt and place on the dinner table with the prow pointing to the nearest body of water, as were the ship burials of old. After dinner, you can fold it up and put it in your pocket!

CRAFT: *SONNENBARKENVOGEL* TABLE LAMP

Meaning "sunship bird," *Sonnenbarkenvogel* is one of those scholarly German loan words that is so much fun to pronounce. It refers to a variation of the ship motif that appeared about the same time as the first boat-shaped graves and was much used to adorn the bronzework of the period. Basically, it's a long ship (a barque) with birds' heads at either end and a sun disc on board.[14]

You will need:

- 1 Ship of the Vanir salt cellar (from the previous craft)
- tea light

To transform your Ship of the Vanir salt cellar into a table lamp, pinch the spirals into teardrops to create outward-

Figure 2

facing birds' heads. Place a tea light on board to represent the sun. See Figure 2.

CRAFT: GREENING CANDLES

This craft begins with store-bought tapers. The darkening shades of green wax symbolize the reawakening of the earth. The candles can serve as the focal point of a formal Walpurgis dinner table.

You will need:

- white taper candles, preferably still joined by the wicks
- paraffin
- green concentrated candle dye
- coffee can
- fairly deep cooking pot
- dowels or chopsticks—how many depends on how many candles you are going to dip

Break up about two pounds of paraffin blocks and put them in the coffee can. Place the coffee can in a pot half-filled with water and heat until the wax has melted. Keep the water hot but not boiling. Following the instructions

on the package, add your concentrated candle dye to the melted wax. It should turn the wax a mellow forest green.

Hang the first pair of tapers on one of the dowels and dip them into the wax. You should lower them in almost—but not quite—all the way, so that only the tips of the candles remain white. The rest of the candle should be pale green. Remember, candle-dipping must be done quickly: candle in, candle out. If you leave it in too long, the wax will start to melt off and your candle will come out skinnier than it went in.

After the first dip, hang the candles up, not touching, to cool a little and move on to the next pair. Dip each pair about eight times, lowering less and less of the candle into the wax each time. This way, you will achieve graduated shades of green, beginning with snowy white at the tip and ending with a deeper, more fertile green at the base. Let candles cool thoroughly before using.

CRAFT: CAULDRON FOR A DAY

Many of the giant cauldrons found in bogs and in the graves of ancient priestesses were for ritual use only and were never meant for cooking. You can't cook in this one either, but it's an easy way for the apartment-living witch to set the stage on Walpurgis Night.

Cover the largest bowl you own with aluminum foil, shiny side out. Put three tealights in the bottom of the bowl and light them. Turn off the lights for instant drama. For added effect, surround your cauldron with forsythia, fruit blossoms, pussy willows, or other cuttings with green leaves.

RECIPE: GREEN AND PINK BEANS

As Jack learned, there is no food more magical than beans. The medievals spat them at witches; the Romans threw them at ghosts. This recipe combines canned beans with spring greens to make a hearty dish that will keep everyone going through the night. The following recipe is the "at home" version. If you're planning on cooking over a campfire, you can substitute dry herbs for fresh and add them all together towards the end of cooking. Rinse the beans well—you don't want to add *too* much fuel to the bonfire!

Ingredients:

- 1 can pink beans
- 1 tablespoon olive oil
- 1 clove garlic, minced
- 1½ tablespoons chives
- ½ cup chicken or vegetable stock
- dash tomato juice
- ½ teaspoon dried cilantro
- 1½ tablespoons fresh chervil, chopped

Heat olive oil in a heavy pot. Add garlic and chives. Sauté for about two minutes. Meanwhile, rinse the beans. Add beans, chicken stock, and tomato juice to the pot. Simmer about ten minutes or until a hearty sauce forms. Stir in cilantro and chervil and serve. Goes nicely with broomstick bread (see chapter 6).

RECIPE: APRIL HOPPELPOPPEL

A 1911 Walpurgisnacht menu from the Harz includes "Hoppelpoppel from Satan's vegetable garden."[15] Ordinary *Hoppelpoppel* hails from Berlin. In Berliner dialect, to go *hops* means "to spoil." *Popelig* means "measly." In other words, the dish is a way to use up measly leftovers before they go bad.

This recipe strays from traditional Hoppelpoppel in that it is baked instead of fried, and it contains cheese and spring vegetables. All the ingredients can be found at your grocery store, so there's no need to raid the Devil's potato patch. Because Hoppelpoppel is designed to use up leftovers, feel free to adapt it according to whatever's hanging around in your refrigerator.

Ingredients:

- 6 baby yellow potatoes
- 6 slices bacon
- 1 cup chopped scallions
- 1 cup asparagus tips (save the stalks for Green Soup, chapter 7)
- 4 eggs
- ½ pint heavy cream
- ½ cup grated Gouda or Swiss cheese
- dash salt
- dash black pepper
- dash white wine
- 1 tablespoon chopped chives

Boil the potatoes in a pot of water, taking care not to overcook them. When they're done, run them under cold water. This will make them easier to peel later. Set potatoes aside.

Fry the bacon until crispy, drain on paper towels, and break into bits. Leave a little fat in the pan to fry the scallions.

Fry scallions for 2–3 minutes. Set aside.

Grease 8" x 8" or larger baking dish.

When no longer hot, peel the skins off the potatoes and slice them. Arrange the slices in the baking dish and sprinkle them with a little bit of salt. Add asparagus tips, bacon bits, and scallions.

In a large bowl, beat the eggs and whisk in the cream. Stir in salt, pepper, white wine, and grated cheese. Pour mixture into the baking dish and sprinkle with chives.

Bake at 400°F for 15 minutes. Reduce heat to 350°F and bake for another 15–20 minutes. Let stand about 10 minutes before serving.

RECIPE: BERRY PORRIDGE WITH BROCKEN TOPS AND VANILLA SAUCE

Berry porridge:

In northern Germany, this dessert is known as *Rote Grütze*, literally "red groats," even though it contains no groats.

It can be made with any variety of dark berries and cherries. The Germans usually add red currants, but if you live in a state with a logging industry, you won't be able to get or even grow your own red currants because the plant harbors the destructive white-pine rust.

Ingredients:

1½ cups frozen raspberries
1 cup frozen pitted dark sweet cherries
1½ cups blackberry-cranberry juice or other dark fruit juice
1½ tablespoons sugar
3 tablespoons cornstarch
3 tablespoons water

Put the berries, juice, and sugar in a pot and bring to a boil. While you're waiting, mix the cornstarch and cold water in a cup, stirring until smooth. When the berries boil, stir in the cornstarch and remove from heat. Pour into a serving bowl or six individual dessert bowls. Let cool at room temperature until just warm, then chill in refrigerator several hours.

For a traditional consistency, stir the porridge from time to time to prevent it from setting. If you want a thick pudding, leave it alone.

Top each serving with a Brocken Top and a ring of vanilla sauce (recipes follow).

Brocken Tops:

Ingredients:

3 egg whites (save yolks for vanilla sauce)
⅛ teaspoon cream of tartar
4 tablespoons vanilla sugar (see Cold May punch, chapter 7)

Beat the egg whites and cream of tartar with an electric mixer until soft peaks form. Add the sugar and continue beating until stiff peaks form—i.e., the peaks hold their shapes with

only the very tops flopping over when you lift out the beaters. This is meringue.

Cover a cookie sheet with nonstick foil. Using a largish spoon, drop a scoop of meringue casually but carefully onto the foil so it looks like the snowy peak of a Dr. Seuss mountain. Repeat until meringue is used up.

Bake at 200°F for 1½ hours. Turn off heat and leave in for another 20 minutes. They should be stiff, not spongy. Cool Brocken Tops completely before taking them off the foil. Put them away in a tin and store at room temperature until you're ready to use them. Don't worry about broken Brocken Tops; you can use them in your syllabub. In fact, this recipe makes enough for both the top of the berry porridge and the bottom of the syllabub.

Vanilla sauce:

Ingredients:

½ vanilla bean

1 cup whole milk

2 tablespoons vanilla sugar

3 egg yolks (left over from Brocken Tops)

½ teaspoon cornstarch

With a sharp knife, slit the vanilla bean in half lengthwise and use the tip of the knife to scrape the mark, as the marrow of the bean is called, into a small pot. (Throw the empty pod into your stash of vanilla sugar.) Add milk and sugar and heat until very warm; do not boil.

In a cup, mix the cornstarch with a teensy bit of water. Briskly stir the cornstarch and beaten egg yolks into the vanilla mixture. Continue stirring over low heat until sauce thickens.

If you see bits of cooked egg yolk floating around in your sauce, strain them out before serving. Serve sauce while still warm. If you must make your sauce ahead of time, put a piece of plastic wrap on the surface so no skin can form.

RECIPE: SYLLABUB

Over the course of its history, this English dessert was sometimes drinkable, sometimes spoonable. This one is spoonable. Syllabub was traditionally served on May Eve in Northumberland. A wedding ring was dropped in the cream, and whoever got it was the next to be married.[16]

The earliest syllabubs contained egg white. The addition of the baked meringue is my way of reintroducing the egg white without having to eat it raw. Nor do you have to milk the cream directly from the cow into the bowl as they supposedly did in the seventeenth century.

Ingredients:

- ½ pint whipping cream
- ⅓ cup sugar
- dash white wine
- zest of one lemon
- juice of ½ lemon
- 6 Brocken Tops or small store-bought meringue shells
- pinch nutmeg
- 6 sprigs rosemary

Whip the cream and sugar together with an electric mixer until thick and spoonable. Stir in wine, lemon zest, and lemon juice.

Break up the Brocken Tops in the bottoms of six wine glasses. Spoon the cream on top. Sprinkle with nutmeg and garnish with a sprig of rosemary. If you decide to put a wedding ring in your syllabub, please warn your guests ahead of time!

RECIPE: CUCUMBER SANDWICHES

St. Walburga was, after all, an Englishwoman, so why not put on a high tea in her honor? The cucumber sandwiches can be followed by red-cap cake. Wash it all down with strong black tea—many of your guests will have a long trip ahead of them to the Brocken!

Ingredients:

- ½ seedless cucumber, peeled and sliced very thin
- pinch salt
- 8 slices potato bread—crusts cut off, of course!
- 2 generous tablespoons mayonnaise
- ¼ teaspoon onion powder
- ½ teaspoon dried dill
- dash white or black pepper

Spread the cucumber slices on a paper towel and sprinkle them with salt. In a small bowl, mix mayonnaise, onion powder, dill, and pepper. For each sandwich, spread two slices of bread with mayonnaise mixture, then cover one with cucumber slices, slightly overlapping. Close and cut sandwich into quarters.

RECIPE: RED-CAP CAKE

In England, "Mother Redcap" was a name applied to women believed to be witches. A few Mother Redcaps survived well into the twentieth century. A red cap can also be a frightful kind of ghost that haunts Scottish castles. And then there is Little Redcap, who bears cakes and wine through the forest to her grandmother.

I imagine the raspberries on the top of this cake as a troop of little red-capped pixies who have been invited to help dance away the snows from the crest of the Brocken.

Ingredients:

1 yellow cake mix
oil, eggs, and water (specific amounts depending on cake-mix instructions)
½ teaspoon almond extract
about 4 oz. red currant jam
½ pint heavy cream
¼ cup vanilla sugar (see Cold May punch, chapter 7)
1 teaspoon cornstarch
2 squares white baking chocolate
fresh raspberries

Prepare yellow cake mix according to instructions. Add almond extract to batter, and bake in two layer-cake pans.

When cake is cool, spread bottom layer with jam. If you stir the jam first, it will be easier to spread. Place other layer on top.

Whip the cream, sugar, and cornstarch together at high speed until it's nice and stiff. Spread the cream over the top and sides of the cake.

Arrange the raspberries in a ring on top of the cake. Fill the ring with white chocolate shavings.

Nine

Getting the Coven Together

What is a coven? The word is most probably derived from *covent*, a now obsolete term that comes to us from Latin by way of Old French. It denoted a convent or monastery, a gathering or assembly, as well as an agreement or promise. Not much to do with witches. For the Middle English–speaking Chaucer, a *covent* was a gathering of thirteen people, though not necessarily for nefarious purposes. At some point, *covent* became *coven*, and acquired some very negative connotations indeed.

We may have modern Wicca to thank for *coven*'s triumph over such earlier terms as *coeven* and *coevy*.[1] Coevy no longer has anything to do with witches but denotes instead a flock of birds. You may have deduced by now that both *coven* and *convent* are derived from the same root. Perhaps witches and nuns are not so dissimilar after all!

Today, the word *coven* has come to mean a body of members rather than the place or occasion of their meeting. The

traditional number of members is thirteen: that is, twelve plus one. During the time of the witch trials, that "one" was believed to be the Devil himself or at least a mortal who made himself out to be a devil. The man who took on the role of coven leader, or was accused of so doing, may actually have been impersonating the horned god. The horned god, known as Cernunnos to the Celts, Herne the Hunter to the English, and the Black Huntsman to the medieval Saxons, was a guardian of the animals, an all-important figure in hunter-gatherer societies.

Anyone who has ever taken an elevator to the fourteenth floor knows that Western civilization is still very much at odds with the number thirteen. Is it because witches customarily came in batches of thirteen? Or were covens assigned a membership of thirteen because that number already had such a bad reputation? For Christians, thirteen is the ultimate inauspicious number because it was Judas, the thirteenth guest at the Passover Seder, who betrayed Jesus. The early church fathers believed that by gathering and supping together in groups of thirteen, the witches were thumbing their noses at Jesus and the twelve apostles.[2] In reality, both scripture and coven had drawn the formula of twelve plus one from a far older tradition.

The number three asserts itself again and again (and again!) in the cosmology and social institutions of both Europe and India and many of the lands in between. To the Indo-Europeans, it was the most powerful number of all. The number three encompasses the past, the present, and the future. It represents a beginning, a middle, and an end. Multiply the temporally complete three by the four cardi-

nal directions, and you have the universe. Twelve represents balance and perfection. There are twelve hours in a day and twelve hours in a night. There are twelve days of Christmas. There are twelve months in a year—or are there?

Nowadays, we use the leap year to account for the fact that a solar year—i.e., the amount of time it takes the earth to complete its revolution around the sun—is *about* but not *exactly* 365 days. A lunar year is twelve full cycles of the moon, or 354 days. The lunar year requires even more correction if the months are to continue to fall in their proper seasons.

As a recent archaeological discovery demonstrates, the residents of Bronze Age northern Germany were aware of this discrepancy between the lunar and solar calendars and had figured out a way to manage it. To the twenty-first-century viewer, the Nebra sky disc, as the find has come to be known, looks disturbingly like a winking, bug-eyed smiley face. It was, in fact, an important astronomical tool, its gold plates displaying the positions of sun, moon, and stars in a year when a thirteenth intercalary month was needed.

The Nebra sky disc was unearthed in what is now the state of Saxony-Anhalt, about sixty miles southeast of another famous landmark, the Brocken. In fact, the fabled witches' mountain is clearly visible from the hill under which the disc lay for almost four thousand years.[3] Were the Iron Age Saxons the inheritors of this astronomical know-how? Probably not. Extraneous additions to the disc tell us that its meaning had been lost long before it was buried in

the ground. No longer an observational tool, it had become a mere ritual object.[4]

The black aura that lingers around the number thirteen suggests that, in the Bronze Age imagination, the thirteenth month was considered an unlucky or at least an unstable time. Just as the Nebra sky disc had lost its application, the thirteenth month disappeared from the northern European calendar (though the Chinese still employ it). The *number* thirteen, however, lives on in infamy. Twelve is constant. Add one more and things start to get interesting. If you want interesting things to happen at your Walpurgis Night celebration, consider having thirteen to dinner.

As we have mentioned, *convent* denoted a gathering of people as well as the gathering place. Witches had many such gathering places for, super broomsticks notwithstanding, not all of them could make it to the Brocken. Fortunately, there were lots of other places to choose from.

Blocksberg, an antiquated, alternate name for the Brocken, was originally applied to any mountain where witches were said to meet.[5] About eighty miles north of the Brocken, as the witch flies, is the Lüneberger Heide, or heath, over which witches had been known to prance.[6] There they found plenty of heather and birch for making besoms. Just east of the sea of heather sprawls the ancient Hitzacker chestnut tree. According to legend, the tree's unusual shape is due to the fact that a witch planted it upside down.[7] Perhaps she had imbibed a little too much May wine?

The witches of the Lowlands had to make do with mere hills or the overgrown Bronze Age grave mounds around

which farmers still plow their fields. Lacking these, they could still *convene* upon the barren moor or within the moonlit shadow of an oak.

The Norse World Tree, Yggdrasill, was an ash, but the German version, *Irminsul* or *Yrmensul*,[8] was an oak.[9] Irminsul could be represented by a live oak, such as the sacred one at Geismar, or an oak stump like the one that stood at the center of a pagan cult complex near Marsberg. Don't look for either of these specimens today; both were reduced to splinters, by St. Boniface and Charlemagne respectively, in the eighth century.[10]

When you've all agreed on a place to gather—and it may be your living room—it remains only to find a suitable way to celebrate May Eve. And that's what this chapter is all about. Solitary witches take note: *coven* is ultimately derived from the Latin *conventus*, which means not just an assembly but also an agreement. So if you find yourself the lone witch on the hilltop, rest assured that there are other witches elsewhere who, though not present, are nevertheless in agreement with you. Many of the following crafts and activities are crowd-pleasers, but read on; there is something here for everyone.

ACTIVITY: WHICH WITCH?

If you're going to be brave and celebrate Walpurgis Night with people outside your immediate circle of friends, this game will serve as a good "snow melter" when your guests first arrive.

Prepare a list of well-known witches beforehand, at least one witch for each guest. The witches you choose will

depend on whom you've invited. They must be witches your guests have heard of! Don't throw the first-century Bructeri seeress Veleda into a game for middle-school girls. If you're unsure of the depths of your guests' knowledge, then it's best to stick to television witches and to the witches of Narnia, Oz, Hogwarts, and the Grimms' fairytales. Write the name of each witch on an index card.

As each guest arrives, assign her a witch by pinning or taping an index card to her back. Don't let her see which witch. She must circulate around the room, as everyone else is doing, asking questions about her witch until she has guessed who it is. Only yes or no questions are allowed. "What kind of house do I live in?" is an illegal question. "Hey, do I live in a *gingerbread* house?" is a legal question.

Just so there will be no hard feelings, reserve a special prize for the "loser," that is, the one baffled guest who's interrogated the entire room and still can't guess her witch.

ACTIVITY: GUESSING GAME

It is said that Czech witches cannot enter a house until they have counted every blade of grass on the doorstep. Blades of grass are hard to keep track of, but you can fill a jar with dry beans, green and black jelly beans, beads, or stones, and have each of your friends guess the number as she passes through your door on Walpurgis Night. Give the winner a Witch's Brew pouch, Walpurgis wand, or origami kitchen witch as a prize. The one whose guess is the furthest off can be given the dubious honor of watching over the broomstick bread or rubber-stamping the flying licenses.

Fun with Runes

Runes are one subject that can be taken all too seriously. If you're a runemaster or runologist, then runes are your business and you *must* take them seriously, but that doesn't mean the rest of us can't enjoy them, too. However you intend to use the runes, you should know a little bit about them before you get started.

Rune is derived from an older word related to the modern German *raunen*, "to whisper,"[11] and the Old English *run*, "a secret." Who invented runic writing? The Vikings believed the runes were the gift of the god Odin, who acquired them by dangling for nine days and nights from the World Tree Yggdrasill. Modern scholars insist they were derived from one of the North Italic scripts and were carried north by some far-ranging Germanic tribe such as the Cimbri.[12] The truth may lie somewhere in between.

A few of the twenty-four symbols that make up the Elder Futhark, the oldest runic alphabet, clearly resemble Latin letters. A few more show affinities with other alphabets kicking around the Mediterranean at the time, such as Greek or Etruscan. At least twelve of the runes, however, resemble no other written symbol.[13] Rather than something cobbled together out of foreign sources, runic writing was at least in some part indigenous to the barbarian north.

How old are the runes? The answer is: older than we can know. Their forms tell us that they were designed to be inscribed across the grains of wood or bone.[14] The earliest efforts, therefore, have long ago rotted away, but we do have a few lance shafts, wooden boxes, combs, and bone scrapers that were sunk in bogs as offerings to the gods.[15] They date

to around AD 150. The inscriptions on these objects as well as much later items don't give us a whole lot of information: "Blithgund wrote these runes,"[16] "Rannvieg owns this box,"[17] "Thorfastr made a good comb."[18] (Viking runemasters could run on at length, but I leave discussion of their grandiose memorial stones to the writers of longer books.) Still, the runes give us fascinating little glimpses into lives lived long ago.

It is possible that the runes were the brainchild of one exceptionally bright individual.[19] This real-life Odin may have seen snippets of one of the Italic scripts, then sat down and invented his own system for writing down fleeting thoughts. He may even have been a *she*, for as Blithgund and Rannveig demonstrate, runemaking was not for men only.[20] Such an individual, if he or she existed, may have been a Dane. While the Alpine passages of northern Italy seem the most likely place for the shaping of the runes, the earliest surviving runic inscriptions do not appear anywhere near the Alps. Instead, they are found in Denmark and on the islands of the western Baltic.[21]

Of course, these earliest inscriptions were not in Danish or German or even Old Norse but in an extinct tongue ancestral to all of them. Any but the hardiest scholar would be hard put to pronounce, let alone decipher, such utterances as the one appearing on an ornamental disk from the Danish island of Zealand: "HARIUHA HAITIKA. FARAUISA GIBU AUJA." That is, "Huriuha I am called, who knows dangerous things. I give luck."[22]

In the beginning, the runes or their prototypes were probably not used for writing at all but for divinations, as the Romans observed. They were carved into slivers of wood, sometimes reddened with blood, and used to cast

lots.[23] Often, they were strewn across a white cloth and chosen at random—that is, at the direction of the gods.[24]

The runic alphabet is called the *futhark* due to its first six symbols: Fehu, Uruz, Thurisaz, Ansuz, Raido, and Kaunan. All of the runes have names, and each name has a meaning, as our own *A*, *B*, and *C* once did. Fortunately, these meanings are still known to us, or, rather, they are known to us again. *Un*fortunately, the futhark was not handed down to us all of a piece; it had to be retrieved from scattered references in medieval manuscripts. Other than the order of the runes, not all scholars agree on the results.[25] Since there's still so much we don't know about the runes, don't worry too much about "getting it right" when you're transcribing words and names into the futhark.

To put yourself in the proper mood when you sit down to the making of runes, try reading aloud the poem "Sigrdrífumál" from the *Saga of the Volsungs*. In this poem, the Valkyrie Brynhild imparts to the dragon-slayer Sigurd all she knows "about runes and other matters that concern all things."[26] It's a long poem, to be sure, but worth reading for its beauty and for its intriguing details as Brynhild describes runes cut "on glass and on gold and on the witch's seat,"[27] directing her hero to cut branch runes "on the needles of trees whose limbs lean to the east,"[28] and to cut aid runes on the palm of a woman in childbirth "and hold her hand in yours, and bid the Disir not to fail."[29]

If you find yourself getting restless, however, you can cut to stanza 19, where the Valkyrie sums it up nicely:

These are cure runes
And aid runes

And all ale runes
And peerless power runes
For all to use unspoiled
And unprofaned
To bring about good fortune.
Enjoy them if you have learned them,
Until the gods perish.[30]

CRAFT: THE TOOTHPICK FUTHARK/ RUNIC RUBBINGS

On the following pages is the Elder Futhark, the oldest of the many runic alphabets. To make your own Toothpick Futhark, use flat toothpicks, not the rounded ones. Use whole toothpicks for the long backbones of the runes and break off shorter pieces for the shorter staves. Glue each one down on a piece of paper or cardboard, then lay a piece of white paper over it. Rub the surface with the side of a peeled black crayon. The results will look very ancient indeed. Use your Toothpick Futhark to make invitations or original works of art. Make runic-rubbing place cards and name tags, and see if your guests are able to pick out their own names.

You will need:
- flat toothpicks
- glue
- paper
- black crayon
- and, of course, the runes:

Table 1: The Runes

Symbol	*Sound*	*Name*	*Meaning*
ᚠ	f	Fehu	cattle; wealth in general
ᚢ	oo	Uruz	aurochs: a shaggy wild ox, now extinct
ᚦ	th	Thurisaz	ogre or giant, the *thurse* of Norse mythology
ᚨ	ah	Ansuz	a god, as in "one of the Aesir"
ᚱ	r	Raido	a ride or a wagon; traveling by wheels
ᚲ	k	Kaunan	sickness in general or, more specifically, a cancerous tumor. Fortunately for those whose names begin with *K*, this rune has an alternate name, *Kenaz*, meaning "spill." No, not like spilt milk; a *spill* (*Kien* in German) is a small piece of wood used like a match except it is longer burning. The form of the rune may suggest the bracket, or *Kienspanhalter*, that held the spill in place while it burned.
ᚷ	g	Gebo	gift
ᚹ	w	Wunjo	joy
ᚺ	h	Haglaz	hail, destruction
ᚾ	n	Naudiz	distress or need
ᛁ	ee	Isaz	ice

Symbol	*Sound*	*Name*	*Meaning*
ᛃ	j German y English	Jeran	year, with the connotation that it will be a good one—i.e., one with a good harvest
ᛇ	"eye"	Iwaz	yew tree
ᛈ	p	Pertho	fruit tree; scholars can't agree which one, but pear is a likely candidate
ᛉ	rz	Algiz	This one is usually identified as *elk*, but it has also been suggested that it is the World Tree, Yggdrasill, perhaps originally "Ygrdzil." The sound it makes no longer exists in English or modern German, but you can hear it in names like *Dvorak* and *Urszula.* Algiz appears in the middle of the Old German word for witch, *Hagazussa.*
ᛊ	s	Sowilo	sun
ᛏ	t	Tiwaz	a sky god
ᛒ	b	Berkanan	birch; I've always wondered why this one should stand for birch instead of beech. The German word for "letter" (as in "letter of the alphabet") is *Buchstabe*—literally, "beech stave"—suggesting that the first runes were carved into the bark of beech trees.
ᛖ	eh	Ehwaz	horse

Symbol	*Sound*	*Name*	*Meaning*
ᛗ	m	Mannaz	man or person
ᛚ	l	Laukaz	leek
ᛜ	ng	Ingwaz	*Ing* is another name for the fertility god Frey
ᛞ	d	Dagaz	day
ᛟ	o	Othalan	an inheritance of land

CRAFT: GLITTER RUNES

You will need:

flat toothpicks
stiff paper or cardstock
hole puncher
string
glue
glitter
small paintbrush or cotton swab

In this craft, the toothpick runes themselves are incorporated into the final product. Choose a rune, then cut an oval or circle out of the cardstock. Make it large enough so the rune will fit neatly inside the space. Punch a hole at the top. Glue on your toothpick rune. Brush a little glue onto the toothpicks' surface, being careful not to get any on the paper or card. Sprinkle with glitter, then shake off the excess. Put a string through the hole. You can wear your glitter rune or hang it in the window or from a tree where it can sparkle as it turns in the light. Help visiting witches

make their own glitter runes using the first initials of their names.

ACTIVITY: WITCH WALK

Everyone's used to braking for trick-or-treaters on October 31. Wouldn't it be exciting to see a few witches, goblins, and horned guardians darting among the apple blossoms on April 30? Consider lighting up the warm spring night by taking your revels on the road. A Witch Walk can be as simple or as elaborate, as personal or as private, as you want it to be. Whether you march up the nearest hill with lanterns ablaze or slip unseen through the night, remember: the true spirit of Walpurgis Night is to be found outdoors.

If you want to create order in your procession, arrange yourselves to represent the Three Ages of the Goddess. Crones (and I mean this in the nicest possible sense of the word!) lead the way, followed by the Matrons, with a handful of blushing Maidens bringing up the rear. If you're lucky enough to have equal pairs of men and women, pair off to symbolize the winter and summer halves of the year.

The most important thing, of course, is to get out and experience the magic of the night, but if yours is a particularly creative group, you can choose a theme for your Witch Walk.

The quickest way to explain Walpurgis Night to someone who's never heard of it is, "Halloween in April." Since April 30 is exactly halfway around the year from October 31, you could celebrate by turning Halloween on its head. I've chosen green and black as my Walpurgis colors to symbolize new life rising from the darkness of the earth, but

blue and white are also good candidates because they're the antithesis of Halloween's black and orange. Black encompasses all colors, while white is the absence of color. (When speaking of light, the opposite is true.) Blue is the complement of orange—that is, it appears opposite orange on the color wheel. Consider the visual impact of the quintessential witch with pointy hat and broomstick dressed all in white instead of black. She would, of course, be accompanied by a white cat. Blue paper lanterns can take the place of orange jack-o'-lanterns. And instead of red devils with pitchforks, try green devils with hoes—red and green are also complementary colors.

How about some reverse trick-or-treating while you're out there? You might hand out fennel seedlings as the ancient Greeks used to do in the spring. Or, try a more contemporary, go-green approach, and distribute energy-saving light bulbs. Nowadays, everyone seems to be selling or giving away reusable shopping bags. Why not us Witches? If you can't afford such largesse, consider performing some kind of community service, such as picking up your neighbors' old batteries for recycling. Notify them ahead of time, then be sure to show up in costume on the appointed day.

Help spread the message that the great outdoors begins just there: outdoors. Print up short poems or calling cards (on 100 percent recycled paper, of course) and pop them in people's mailboxes. "The 1st Annual Walpurgis Witch Walk has passed this way and banished King Winter. The witches of ________ remind you to stop and smell the cherry blossoms. Welcome, Spring!"

You don't necessarily have to go the witch route. The members of your coven could dress up to represent a spring story or poem—perhaps one of Goethe's? Comb through Grimm's *Household Stories* for one of the lesser-known fairy-tales like "Mother Hulda" or "The Juniper Tree." Finland's national epic, the *Kalevala*, contains a wonderful story about an old and especially troublesome witch named Louhi who steals the sun and the moon. There are plenty of parts for men in this one, for it's up to the gods Ukko, Ilmarinen, and Vainamoinen to retrieve the celestial bodies, albeit with the help of an airy virgin. With a little inspiration and a few creative thinkers and ambitious artist types, you could have a real event!

CRAFT/ACTIVITY: WITCH BOXES

In this craft, Joseph Cornell meets the cunning man meets the modern witch. The twentieth-century artist Joseph Cornell was famous for his three-dimensional assemblages. You will soon be famous for your witch boxes.

The witch boxes that common folk bought from traveling salesmen in eighteenth-century England contained, or were supposed to contain, bits of human bone along with more pleasant components such as dried herbs and scraps of rowan wood. The contents were displayed under glass covers, so buyers could be sure they were getting what they paid for. The boxes were meant to keep witches away rather than attract them.

Here we turn the tables on the witch-hunters and create boxes of our own to attract good luck, good spirits, and good times. There are no hard and fast rules for assembling

a witch box. First, line the box with the paper(s) of your choice. Using torn scraps of different kinds of paper will make for greater visual interest. Take your time arranging the objects inside before gluing them down. Ideas will suggest themselves to you as you work. When you're ready, glue the pieces in place securely enough that you can hang your witch box on the wall.

If you're planning to do this with a group, provide the participants with a wish list ahead of time so you'll all have a variety of materials to work with. Suggestions follow:

- Small, shallow boxes: e.g., the kind that small chocolate assortments come in
- Candle stubs: You can use any kind of candle stubs. I like the small, red "angel chime" candles that are sold at Christmastime. All over the world, red has been regarded as a protective color, especially against plague. Besides, I don't like to throw my Christmas candle stubs away. This is a way to give them new life as art.
- Joss paper: You should be able to find this relatively inexpensive gilded paper in a Chinatown near you, or in a Chinese grocery store with a large non-food section. Look for it near the incense. Also known as "ghost money," it is burned at funerals and at graveside rituals. Himalayan bark paper, marbled paper, or Japanese washi will also make a pretty lining for your witch box.
- Incense sticks, cotton balls, clay: Stick the incense in the clay while it's still moldable. Glue wisps of cotton balls to the tips of the incense sticks to create "smoke."

- Thin yarn, round toothpicks (both the short and the long "party" kind): Most of us, in the United States at least, learn how to make an *ojo de Dios,* or "God's eye," in elementary school. If you didn't, the technique is simple. Glue two toothpicks together to make a cross. Beginning at the very center of the cross, start winding the yarn from arm to arm. Soon, a diamond will appear.
- Pine needles for binding onto party toothpicks to make tiny besoms as in the origami kitchen witch (chapter 5)
- Juniper twigs, sage leaves, plus any other herbs you have around: Make teeny tiny smudge sticks to incorporate into your witch boxes. (See Walpurgis wand, chapter 7.)
- Tiny mirrors, shiny paper, or cardboard; jingle bells: both of these are traditionally used to deflect or confuse evil spirits
- Dried or artificial flowers
- Dried or artificial berries, especially red ones to represent the rowan
- Interesting pebbles
- Interesting twigs
- Glitter
- Anything else you can think of!

ACTIVITY: WITCH ELECTIONS

In the town of Oberwesel, on the Rhine, *Walpurgisnacht* is *Weinhexennacht*, or "Wine-Witch Night." Each year on April 30, the new Wine-Witch, chosen by the local vintners, pops out of a giant wine barrel in the market square.[31] Arrayed in medieval hennin and a lace-trimmed, claret-colored gown, the Wine-Witch then presides over the night's revels.[32]

Most of us don't live in wine country, but every city, town, and village is known for *something*. A Seattle-based coven might elect a Coffee Witch. Washington DC witches could choose a Cherry Blossom Witch. Southwestern covens might be interested in the idea of a Chili Witch. If you live far enough to the north that on April 30 it's still too cold to look for many signs of spring, how about a Chilly Witch?

Think your town has nothing to recommend it? Most of today's Madisons and Springfields once had more interesting names. The town where I live used to be called Turkey Town, so I think a Turkey Witch would be in order, but so far I haven't found anyone to agree with me. If your town has or had a Native American name, find out what it means. It might inspire you. Elect a witch to draw attention to an ecological issue or a threatened species—e.g., a Watershed Witch, Wetlands Witch, or Big Brown Bat Witch. The costume you make for your elected witch doesn't have to be as fancy as the Oberwesel Wine-Witch's. It could be as simple as a crown of apple or forsythia blossoms, a sash of braided garlic, or a turkey feather hair-tie.

How to choose your Very Special Witch? You can draw names out of a cauldron on Walpurgis Night or ask your coven for nominations ahead of time. Hold the election itself on Walpurgis Night by casting glitter runes.

CRAFT: CRAYON CANDLES

If you grew up during the 1970s, you've probably made a dribbly candle out of melted crayons. This is not that craft. But it is a fun one to do with kids.

You will need:

- candles in assorted colors—mold-made or pillar candles are better than dipped tapers for this craft
- construction paper in assorted colors
- black marker
- glue

Choose a candle and sheet of construction paper in a matching color. Trim the paper so you can wrap it once around the candle like a crayon label. With the black marker, decorate the paper to make it look like a real crayon label. Make up a name for your color and neatly print it on the label. Here are a few suggestions: Walburga White, Faustian Fuschia, Goethe Green, Rowanberry Red, Huntsman Black, Wolf's Eye Yellow, and Bertha Blue.

Wrap the label around the candle and glue it at the seam. Don't forget to peel the paper down as the candle burns!

Eleventh-Hour Costumes

On Walpurgis Night, most German "witches" can get away with a kerchief, shawl, and twig broom. Here are a few more quick and easy ideas:

- Pull on a white T-shirt so the neck of the T-shirt frames your face. Leave your arms out. Now, pull a black sweatshirt or long-sleeved T-shirt on over the first so the white peeks out only at your forehead. Look in the mirror, and you will see the bewimpled image of St. Walburga looking back.
- Use birch twigs and floral tape to make a crown for your head. Put strips of black electrical tape on white clothing to simulate birch bark. You're the primeval spirit that resides in the birch tree.
- Got a red cap? Go as a red-cap!
- Thread some juniper berries on a string to make a necklace and transform yourself into Frau Wacholder. You can spend the evening telling everyone the unvarnished truth.
- Hot-glue one or more pocket flashlights onto a plastic hairband. In the dark, you'll look like a will-o'-the-wisp.
- Two ways to recognize witches on Walpurgis Night were to wear a crown of ivy leaves or to pin a wild radish on your clothing.[33]
- Our old friend Jacob Grimm tells us that one way to get in with the witches on Walpurgis Night is to walk backwards into a crossroads with your clothes on inside out.

If you use this for a costume idea, you should probably leave out the walking backwards part.

CRAFT/ACTIVITY: WALPURGIS WISHES

No one is busier on Walpurgis Night than Freya. As a fertility goddess, she initiates that fertility by bringing together man and woman. Under cover of darkness on May Eve, the unmarried youths of the village went courting, not with flowers and chocolate but with birch or fir saplings they had cut down in the forest themselves. The boys then decked the trees with ribbons and stuck them in the ground outside their girlfriends' houses. The appearance of one of these decorated trees, or *Liebesmaien*, in front of a girl's house could, sometimes, even be interpreted as a proposal of marriage.[34] Here we have a very public display of affection.

Walpurgis Night, along with practically every other saint's day in the calendar, gave even the girls who had not been honored with a Liebesmaien a chance to know something about her potential future husband. Shake a fruit tree on Walpurgis Night. Do you hear dogs barking? Your intended will come from the direction the dogs are barking.[35] Or, hang a length of thread behind a picture of the Virgin Mary. Leave it there for three days. Take the thread down on Walpurgis Night and have each girl in the household tie a knot in it. At midnight, untie the knots and, with eyes closed, pull the thread tight, entreating Walburga to show you your future husband. Open your eyes and let the thread go. The twisting of the fibers should tell each of you what sorts of fellows your husbands will be.[36] If this is too much

trouble, then go out to the village gate on Walpurgis Night. Ask the first name of the first person you meet. That is the name of your future partner.[37]

This last trick works for both sexes, but for the most part, there was a definite double standard on Walpurgis Night. Village boys could impress their sweethearts by leaping high over the fire or planting phallic professions of their love at their doors. For the boys, this was an empowering occasion. Girls, however, could wish only for a hint about whom they would be saddled with. One explanation may be that males, in popular imagination, could not see into the future, whereas females, more closely associated with Freya, the practice of seid, and the Norns (as illustrated by the use of the thread),[38] could. Still, it is with a sense of relief that we leave certain of the old customs behind.

Whether it's the Liebesmaien placed before a sweetheart's door or the imposing *Maibaum* erected on the village green, it has been a tradition to chip away at the forest on Walpurgis Night. England has its "nail trees" and "rag trees," France its *chêne à clous* (literally, "studded oak"), on which petitioners of the otherworldly powers-that-be still attach nails, clothes, shoes, rosaries, and medical paraphernalia. Although this is done while the tree is still standing, the practice has its downside; after many years, the tree becomes so smothered by offerings that it has to be burnt.[39]

The following activity is more eco-friendly than those mentioned above. Find a healthy tree in your neighborhood or deep within the woods. It should be one that won't mind having a few paper packets hanging from it for the duration of the year. Now, make a wish. What do you want

for yourself between now and the next Walpurgis Night? Acceptance to college? A new job? A soulmate? Before you forget your wish, jot it down on a scrap of paper. Then stow it safely and secretly, following the instructions below. As always, be careful what you wish for!

You will need:

- one 8 x 8-inch square of durable yet flexible paper, such as Himalayan bark paper or Japanese *washi*
- thin yarn or thick perle cotton (since color changes are difficult, a variegated yarn is nice)

Fold your square of paper in half diagonally, then in half again. Unfold. The creases will show you your center point. Fold all corners in to the center point. Unfold and write your wish in the center square. Insert any flat, lightweight good luck charms before folding the points back in to the center. Fold all points to the center twice more so you are left with a three-inch-square packet of paper. You may want to tape the edges before going on to the next step so they won't pop open; you can remove the tape later.

Without cutting it from the ball or skein, tie the yarn crosswise around the paper packet as if you are wrapping a present. Knot the yarn and cut one end short but leave the other very long, about three feet. The crossed strings will function just like the toothpick or popsicle stick cross around which a God's eye, or ojo de Dios, is woven. Take the long end of your yarn in hand and pass it over, then under the first arm of the cross. Pass it on over the neighboring arm, under and over to the next arm, and so on. You will soon see a diamond appear.

It's a little trickier than making a God's eye with popsicle sticks, because the yarn is yielding, but you'll soon get the hang of it. Press your thumb over the center of the cross to keep the pattern neat.

When you've reached the edge of your paper square, you can pass the yarn to the back and knot off.

If you're worried your Walpurgis wish might be disturbed, climb up into the branches and hang it where it won't be seen. If your wish comes true by next Walpurgis Night, be sure to leave a gift for the tree spirit who watched over it all year.

Conclusion
The True Witch

Our journey through Walpurgis Night has come to an end. The fires have all died down, though there is still a whiff of juniper smoke in the air. Most of the witches have either walked or flown home, their servants bearing their empty cauldrons. The Valkyries, in the shape of ravens, have been driven off from the leavings of the feast, the Wolf Crones loping beside them. The *Alraune* has retreated to her cupboard, the Elder Mother to her teapot. The *Drude* has retired to the blanket chest, and the *Bilwis*—was it even invited?—has gone back to cutting the grass. The hags will stay on in the mountains, but we won't hear from them again until the next snowfall. The weather witches have hidden their lightning bolts under their cloaks and faded into the dawn, recalled by Mother Hulda.

There will be only fair weather today for the picnickers emerging from their houses with baskets full of strawberries and May wine. The sun is shining. Walpurgis Night is already half forgotten.

The witches, too, have been forgotten, but they are not actually gone, for a true witch can make herself at home just about anywhere: in a lone dogwood on a suburban front lawn, in a pocket of weeds in the corner of a parking lot, in a stand of birches at the edge of the railroad tracks. On May Day morning, still radiant from the glow of last night's fires, the true witch disappears into the bark of her tree—cloak, kerchief, broomstick, and all.

There she passes the year gazing at the moon, dancing to the scraping of the branches, and slipping out now and then to tend her wild garden. She plaits herself a crown of dandelions at Midsummer and laughs herself silly at Halloween, perhaps even frightening a few of the neighborhood children. The snow falls and she looks forward, in her own way, to Christmas.

As the winter drags on, the true witch becomes a bent and withered crone, her face as deeply lined as the bark of the tree in which she hides. The tree, too, will one day grow old and die or fall before the axe of urban renewal, but the witch will be all right. She will fly or hobble away and make herself a new home, knowing all the while that on the Night of the Witches, she will be young again.

Endnotes

Chapter One

1. Todd, *Everyday Life of the Barbarians*, 10.
2. Frazer, *The Golden Bough*, 649.
3. Guiley, *The Encyclopedia of Witches and Witchcraft*, 357.
4. Summers, *The Geography of Witchcraft*, 519.
5. Jacob, *A Witch's Guide to Gardening*, 53.
6. Porteous, *The Forest in Folklore and Mythology*, 256–57.
7. Jacob, 107.
8. Mercatante, *The Magic Garden*, 4.
9. Guiley, 70.
10. Steiger, *Real Ghosts, Restless Spirits and Haunted Places*, 395.

Chapter Two

1. Guiley, 123.
2. Grimm, *Teutonic Mythology, Volume III*, 1051.

3. Ibid., 1050–52.
4. Ashliman, "Witchcraft Legends."
5. Ibid.
6. Harvey, "Season of the Witch: Walpurgisnacht in Germany's Harz Mountains."
7. Guiley, 123.
8. Harvey, "Season of the Witch."
9. Russ, *German Festivals and Customs*, 57.
10. Cooper, *Mendelssohn, Goethe and the Walpurgis Night*, 13.
11. Cooper, 14.
12. Cooper, 13.
13. Brothers Grimm, *The German Legends of the Brothers Grimm*, 247–48.
14. Goethe, *Faust*, 104.

Chapter Three

1. Jacob, 111.
2. Davidson, *The Lost Beliefs of Northern Europe*, 115–16.
3. Brothers Grimm, *Household Stories*, 128–31.
4. Davidson, *Gods and Myths of Northern Europe*, 125–26.
5. Baroja, *The World of the Witches*, 53–54.
6. Russ, 58.
7. Ibid.
8. Schulte-Peevers, "Witches, Trains and Half Timber–The Magic of the Harz," 34.
9. Russ, 58–59.
10. Goethe, *Faust*, 219.

Chapter Four

1. Casanova, "St. Walburga."
2. Redlich, "Walburga of Heidenheim," 606.
3. Santino, *Halloween and Other Festivals of Life and Death*, xix.
4. Jones and Pennick, *A History of Pagan Europe*, 160.
5. Casanova.
6. Redlich, 607.
7. Irwin, *Context and Text: Method in Liturgical Theology*, 73.
8. Kuhns, *The Habit*, 75–78.
9. Ibid., 53.
10. Ibid., 77.
11. Irwin, 72.
12. Redlich, 769.
13. Casanova.
14. Ferguson, *The Vikings: A History*, 48–51.
15. Hodge, "Waelburga and the Rites of May."
16. Ibid.
17. Seymour, *The Forgotten Arts and Crafts*, 372.
18. Berger, *The Goddess Obscured*, 64.
19. Davidson, *The Lost Beliefs of Northern Europe*, 116.
20. Keightley, *The World Guide to Gnomes, Fairies, Elves, and Other Little People*, 474.
21. Berger, 127.
22. Ibid., 55–70.
23. Turner and Coulter, *The Dictionary of Ancient Deities*, 343.

24. Todd, *Everyday Life of the Barbarians*, 128–29.
25. Davidson, 14.
26. Ibid., 133.
27. Berger, 64.
28. Gardner, *Gods, Goddesses, and Mythology*, 992.
29. Ibid., 992.
30. Davidson, 118.
31. Leeming, *The Oxford Companion to World Mythology*, 407.
32. Hodge.
33. "Walburga," *Patron Saints Index.*
34. Rätsch, *Walpurgisnacht*, 17.
35. Herrmann, *Deutsche Mythologie*, 285.
36. Irwin, 72.
37. Casanova.
38. Guiley, 349.
39. Casanova.
40. Ott, "Oil of Saints."

Chapter Five

1. Preussler, *The Little Witch*, 12.
2. Baroja, 123.
3. Russell and Alexander, *A History of Witchcraft*, 55.
4. Russell and Alexander, 46.
5. Ibid.
6. Porteous, 166.
7. Sturluson, *Heimskringla: or, Lives of the Norse Kings*, 7.

8. Leach, ed., *Funk and Wagnalls Standard Dictionary of Folklore, Mythology and Legend*, vol. I, 40.
9. Scherf, *Zauberpflanzen, Hexenkräuter*, 72.
10. Leach, 672.
11. Ibid., 670.
12. Scherf, 73.
13. Baroja, 50.
14. Leach, 671.
15. Mercatante, 143.
16. Scherf, 73.
17. Leach, 40.
18. Ibid.
19. Leach, 671.
20. Guiley, 8.
21. Porteous, 93.
22. Mercatante, 3–4.
23. Ibid., 4.
24. Petzoldt, "Spirits and Ghosts," 393.
25. Grimm, *Teutonic Mythology, Volume II*, 475–76.
26. Turner and Coulter, 101.
27. Beckmann and Beckmann, *Das geheime Wissen der Kräuterhexen*, 131.
28. Grimm, 474–75.
29. Russell and Alexander, 12.
30. Dashu, "Kings Against Witches."
31. Davidson, *Gods and Myths of the Viking Age*, 117.
32. Baroja, 47.
33. Maple, *The Dark World of Witches*, 164–70.

34. Russell and Alexander, 76.
35. Scherf, 37.
36. Ibid., 71.
37. Ibid., 81.
38. Grimm, *Teutonic Mythology, Volume I*, 422–23.
39. Skott, "Easter Witches in Sweden."
40. Luleå University, " 'Pask'—Easter."
41. Ibid.
42. Porteous, 90.
43. Jacob, 53.
44. Grimm, *Teutonic Mythology, Volume IV*, 1819.
45. Andersen, *Tales from Hans Andersen.*
46. Jacob, 15.
47. Guiley, 147.
48. Davidson, *The Lost Beliefs of Northern Europe*, 111.
49. Guiley, 147.
50. Ibid.
51. Jacob, 33.
52. Davidson, *Gods and Myths of Northern Europe*, 65–66.
53. Branston, *The Lost Gods of England*, 104.
54. Magnusson and Palsson, trans., *Njal's Saga*, 349–51.
55. Branston, 98.
56. Davidson, *The Lost Beliefs of Northern Europe*, 119.
57. Branston, 103.
58. Baroja, 124.
59. Grimm, *Teutonic Mythology, Volume III*, 1088.
60. Ogilvie and Pálsson, "Weather and Witchcraft in the Sagas of Icelanders."

61. Ogilvie and Pálsson, 4.
62. Magnusson and Hermann Palsson, 61, 68.
63. Ibid.
64. Ibid.
65. Guiley, 323.
66. Grimm, 1088.
67. Ibid.
68. Davidson, *The Lost Beliefs of Northern Europe*, 116.
69. Grimm Brothers, *Household Stories by the Brothers Grimm*, 129.
70. Grimm, 1088.
71. Stock, "Wild Woman," 435.
72. Russell and Alexander, 50.
73. Ibid., 46–48.
74. Ibid., 49.
75. Porteous, 92.
76. Baroja, 137–38.
77. Davidson, *The Lost Beliefs of Northern Europe*, 137.
78. Thorsson, ed., *The Sagas of Icelanders: A Selection*, 658.
79. Davidson, *Gods and Myths of Northern Europe*, 120.
80. Thorsson, 658.
81. Ibid.
82. Davidson, *Gods and Myths of Northern Europe*, 118.
83. Ibid., 120.
84. Maple, 26–28.
85. Porteous, 87.
86. Baroja, 48.
87. Jackson, *Traditional Epics*, 363.

88. Jacob, 18.
89. Mallory and Mair, *The Tarim Mummies*, 220.
90. Ibid., 196–97.
91. Barber, *The Mummies of Urumchi*, 199.
92. Mallory and Mair, 220.
93. Barber, 200.
94. Guiley, 381.

Chapter Six

1. Jacob, 15.
2. Baroja, 90.
3. Guiley, 357.
4. Rätsch, 15.
5. Guiley, 34.
6. Rätsch, 51.
7. Seymour, 318–19.
8. Ibid., 33.
9. Wilbur, *Indian Handicrafts*, 112–13.
10. Mercatante, 3–4.
11. Jacob, 106.
12. Ibid., 21.
13. Ibid., 18.
14. Pickering, *Cassell's Dictionary of Superstitions*, 238.
15. Ibid., 237.
16. Ibid., 83.
17. Talbot and Whiteman, *Brother Cadfael's Herb Garden*, 195.
18. Mercatante, 69.

19. Talbot and Whiteman, 195.
20. Ibid., 195.
21. Pickering, 88.
22. Ibid., 89.
23. Richard Kieckhefer, "Witchcraft," in Lindahl et al., 438.
24. Thonger, *A Calendar of German Customs*, 43.
25. Pickering, 89–90.
26. Guiley, 34.
27. Summers, *The Geography of Witchcraft*, 520.
28. Pickering, 89.
29. Ibid., 88–89.
30. Ibid., 89.
31. Baroja, 35.
32. Thonger, 41.
33. Guiley, 248.
34. Baroja, 123.

Chapter Seven

1. Sanders, *Hedgemaids and Fairy Candles*, 181.
2. Talbot and Whiteman, 197.
3. Kamm, *Old-Time Herbs for Northern Gardens*, 155.
4. Talbot and Whiteman, 184.
5. Scherf, 71.
6. Ibid., 97.
7. Ibid.
8. Leach, 441.
9. Scherf, 23.
10. Kamm, 155.

11. Scherf, 124.
12. Sanders, 67–68.
13. Scherf, 158.
14. Jacob, 106.
15. Ibid., 11.
16. Talbot and Whiteman, 57.
17. Sturluson, *Heimskringla: or, Lives of the Norse Kings*, 186.
18. Rausch and Lotz, *Dumont's Lexicon of Herbs*, 46.
19. Guiley, 147.
20. Rausch and Lotz, 226.
21. Ibid., 227.
22. Ibid., 229.
23. Kamm, 93.
24. Scherf, 170.
25. Stephen O. Glosecki, "Shamanism," in Lindahl, et al., 378–79.
26. Scherf, 170.
27. Glosecki, 379.
28. Scherf, 170–71.
29. Ibid., 170.
30. Ibid., 170–71.
31. Rausch and Lotz, 30.
32. Talbot and Whiteman, 12.
33. Rausch and Lotz, 53.
34. Ibid.
35. Ibid.
36. Talbot and Whiteman, 84.

37. Kamm, 102.
38. Talbot and Whiteman, 98.
39. Leach, 313.
40. Talbot and Whiteman, 98.
41. Kamm, 88.
42. Talbot and Whiteman, 103.
43. Kamm, 87.
44. Ibid., 87–92.
45. Talbot and Whiteman, 103.
46. Kamm, 92.
47. Ibid., 67–68.
48. Barber, "Spinning and Weaving," in Lindahl, et al., 390.
49. Leach, 393.
50. Ibid.
51. Talbot and Whiteman, 105.
52. Leach, 393.
53. Talbot and Whiteman, 105.
54. Leach, 393.
55. Boyer, *Tree-Talk: Memories, Myths and Timeless Customs*, 58.
56. Metzger, ed., *Culinaria Germany*, 201.
57. Porteous, 93–94.
58. Leach, 562–63.
59. Sanders, 171.
60. Ibid.
61. Talbot and Whiteman, 143.
62. Woll, *Feste und Bräuche im Jahreslauf*, 66.
63. Sanders, 171.

64. Kamm, 104.
65. Sanders, 171.
66. Talbot and Whiteman, 168.
67. Kamm, 167.
68. Leach, 957.
69. Kamm, 169.
70. Leach, 957.
71. Rausch and Lotz, 238–41.
72. Kamm, 169.
73. Ibid., 170.
74. Leach, 957.
75. Kamm, 172.
76. Thompson, *Holiday Symbols*, 639.
77. Jacob, 112.
78. Rausch and Lotz, 247.
79. Mercatante, 144.
80. Jacob, 113–15.
81. Fiske, *Myths and Myth-Makers*, 100.
82. Rausch and Lotz, 246.
83. Mercatante, 144.
84. Kamm, 71.
85. Leach, 960.
86. Talbot and Whiteman, 169.
87. Kamm, 77.
88. Jacob, 12.
89. Kamm, 77.
90. Jacob, 64.
91. Borden and Coyote, "The Smudging Ceremony," 55.

92. Rausch and Lotz, 253.
93. Kamm, 191.
94. Ibid.
95. Rausch and Lotz, 126.
96. Ibid., 128.
97. Kamm, 192.

Chapter Eight

1. Prague TV, "Witches' Night."
2. Fernández-Armesto, ed., *The Times Guide to the Peoples of Europe*, 253.
3. Lazarová, "Witch-Burning Night Brings Record Number of Fires."
4. Lazarová, "Magazine" (May 5, 2007).
5. Lazarová, "Magazine" (April 29, 2006).
6. Johnston, "Czechs Celebrate 'Čarodějnice'—An Annual Witch-Burning Festival."
7. Kubik, "Czech—Witches—Accident."
8. Cunliffe, *Europe Between the Oceans: 1900 BC—AD 1000*, 258–60.
9. Anthony Harding, "Reformation in Barbarian Europe, 1300–600 BC," in *The Oxford Illustrated Prehistory of Europe*, 318–19.
10. Cunliffe, 260.
11. Davidson, *The Lost Beliefs of Northern Europe*, 19–20.
12. Jones and Pennick, *A History of Pagan Europe*, 145.
13. Sturluson, *The Viking Gods*, 33–37.
14. Cunliffe, 258–59.

15. Russ, 58.
16. Daniels and Stevans, *Encyclopedia of Superstitions, Folklore and the Occult Sciences of the World, Volume II*, 1540.

Chapter Nine

1. Guiley, 66.
2. Jacob,19.
3. Cramer, "The World Is a Disk: The Sky of Nebra—Germany's 3,600-Year-Old Astronomical Clock," 10–12.
4. Ibid.
5. Grimm, *Teutonic Mythology, Volume IV*, 1619.
6. Beckmann and Beckmann, 149.
7. Boyer, 36.
8. Grimm, *Teutonic Mythology, Volume I*, 116.
9. Porteous, 193–94.
10. Cooper, 9.
11. Fischer-Fabian, *Die ersten Deutschen*, 119.
12. Robinson, *Old English and Its Closest Relatives*, 94.
13. Todd, *The Early Germans*, 118.
14. Lavold, *Viking Patterns for Knitting*, 192.
15. Robinson, 95.
16. Jones and Pennick, 153.
17. Campbell, et al., 103.
18. Ibid.
19. Robinson, 94.
20. Jones and Pennick, 153.
21. Robinson, 94.

22. Fischer-Fabian, 119–120.
23. Davidson, *The Lost Beliefs of Northern Europe*, 99.
24. Jones and Pennick, 115.
25. Robinson, 93.
26. Byock, trans., *The Saga of the Volsungs*, 70.
27. Ibid., 70.
28. Ibid., 69.
29. Ibid.
30. Ibid., 70.
31. "Weinhexennacht," oberwesel.de
32. "Wein-Hexennacht in Oberwesel am Rhein."
33. Daniels and Stevens, 1540.
34. Woll, 51.
35. "Walpurgisnacht im Harz: Hexenzauber und Liebesorakel."
36. Rätsch, 42.
37. "Walpurgisnacht im Harz: Hexenzauber und Liebesorakel."
38. Rätsch, 42
39. Boyer, 53–67.

Glossary

Aesir: One of two families of Norse deities. Headed by Odin and Frigga, the Aesir dwell in the heavenly realm of Asgard and are associated with the sky, weather, and war. Notable members of the Aesir clan include Thor, Tyr, and Balder.

Alemanns: A confederacy of Germanic tribes arising in what is now southwestern Germany in the early third century AD. Their name means "all men." Loosely organized under a number of kings and princes, their eclipse by the Franks was complete by the early eighth century. There are plenty of "witches" among the Alemanns' descendants in Germany and Switzerland, but they make their appearance during Carnival season rather than Walpurgis Night.

Ash Wednesday: The first day of Lent, when the palms from Palm Sunday are burnt and smeared on the foreheads of parishioners. In Protestant Iceland, Ash Wednesday

became an excuse for all sorts of pranks involving bags of ashes or stones and even dead cats and ravens.

Bel: A Celtic god of light, also called *Belenus* and sometimes *Bil.*

Beltane: The Irish name of the Celtic festival celebrated on or about May 1. It is marked by the lighting of fires on hilltops. While Beltane has much in common with the Germanic observance of Walpurgis Night, the Celts saved the more ghoulish aspects for Samhain (the forerunner of our modern Halloween).

Benedictine: An order of Catholic monks and nuns who live according to the rule established by St. Benedict (c. 480–c. 547). In the early days, the Benedictines were known for their flowing black robes.

Bertha: Folkloric figure known also as Perchta and more or less identical to Holda. Bertha is the aspect of the earth Goddess most strongly associated with spring. *See also* Freya, Frigga, Holda.

besom: A twig broom.

Bil: Norse goddess of the waning moon.

Blocksberg: Another name for the Brocken, or for any of several German mountains on which witches were said to gather. *See also* Brocken.

Bohemia: A region that is now the western Czech Republic, named for the Celtic Boii tribe who dwelt there during the Iron Age. The culture of Bohemia reflects its history as a crossroads of Celtic, Germanic, and Slavic influences.

Brocken: The highest peak of the Harz mountain range in north-central Germany, on which witches were said to

gather, especially on the night of April 30. In Germany, it was also known as *Blocksberg*; the Swedish equivalent is *Blåkulla* or *Blockula*.

broom squire: A professional broom-maker.

Bructeri: An early Germanic tribe. The most famous of the Bructeri was the seeress Veleda, who, around 78 AD, negotiated for peace between her people and Rome. The Bructeri lived in what is now the Rhineland region of Germany.

Celts: A widespread Indo-European-speaking people whose language and culture persists principally in Ireland, the British Isles, and Brittany in France. The first culture to be identified as "Celtic" was the Hallstatt Culture, which arose in Austria around 800 BCE.

Charlemagne: "Charles the Great," king of the Franks and later Holy Roman Emperor. Born 742, died 814.

corn dolly: A human figure made from straw left over from the harvest. A corn dolly can also be any plaited or woven straw figure. Corn dollies were, and sometimes still are, used to represent the grain goddess.

coven: An organized body of witches, usually thirteen in number, the thirteenth of which serves as the leader.

crone: A wrinkled old woman. The crone epitomizes the withering, winter phase of the earth Goddess. The word *crone* can also refer to an aged ewe.

Cross-Quarter Days: Holy days falling roughly halfway between the solar events of solstice and equinox. They are February 2, May 1, August 1, and November 1. *See also* Imbolc, Beltane, Walpurgis Night, Lammas, Samhain.

crozier: A staff with a curlicue on top. Croziers were carried by bishops, abbots, and abbesses. The crozier was modelled after the shepherd's crook, a long cane used to keep sheep in line.

Druids: The priestly class of the Celtic Britons and Gauls. As well as presiding over rituals, they also served as teachers and judges.

Floralia: The Roman celebration of spring, taking place in late April and early May and dedicated to the goddess of flowers.

Franks: A confederacy of at least four Germanic tribes, including the Bructeri, who came to dominate much of what is now France and Germany in about 400 AD. The Franks are known for the rich grave goods with which they buried their kings and queens. (The award for best fashion sense among the Franks goes to King Childeric, who, upon his death in 482, was interred in a cloak covered with three hundred gold and garnet bees.) The Franks converted to Christianity early in the Migration Period. The forced conversion of other tribes reached its height under the Frankish king Charlemagne. *See also* Charlemagne, Migration Period.

Franks Casket: An ornately carved box that was neither made by nor ever belonged to the Franks. Rather, it was for a time in the possession of one Sir Augustus Franks. Of Anglo-Saxon workmanship, the Franks Casket has something for everyone: runic and Latin inscriptions along with scenes from Roman history, the New Testament, and Old English poetry. An inscription on the

front of the casket informs us, in riddle form, that it was carved from the bones of a beached whale.

Frey: The principal god of the Vanir in Norse mythology. He is concerned with the fertility of the fields, as well as death, ships, and the sea. *See also* Vanir, Freya.

Freya: Norse goddess of love, fertility, and death. Freya is the sister of Frey. Both are prominent members of the family of gods known as the Vanir. *See also* Frey, Frigga, Vanir.

Frigga: A goddess of Norse mythology, wife of Odin, mother and queen of the family of gods known as the Aesir. In Teutonic mythology, Frigga is indistinguishable from the fertility goddess Freya. *See also* Aesir, Freya.

futhark: The runic alphabet, named for its first six symbols.

Gallic: Relating to the Celtic inhabitants of Gaul (now France).

Germanic: Originally, a classification given by the Romans to those barbarians living to the north and east of the river Rhine and who remained resistant to Roman rule. These early "Germans" certainly did not regard themselves as Germanic; instead, they would have identified themselves as members of a number of small, interrelated tribes. Nowadays, the term *Germanic* also refers to a group of languages that includes, among others, English, German, Dutch, and Swedish.

gilly flower: A wallflower or wild carnation.

God's eye: A charm made of two crossed sticks wrapped with yarn in a diamond shape. Indigenous people in Mexico make amulets composed of multiple God's eyes,

or *ojos de Dios*, wrapped in brightly colored yarn. The same technique is used to wrap the paper amulets and spirit catchers of Nepal. In Japan, the God's eye design is embroidered on toy balls called *temari*. *See also* spirit catcher.

Gothic: A more or less Germanic people who traced their origins back to southern Scandinavia but did not come to prominence until they had reached the shores of the Black Sea. Eventually, they spread throughout the Roman Empire and beyond. The far-ranging Goths brought together the Germanic, Roman, Byzantine, and Central Asian styles that would later characterize "Gothic" architecture. Interestingly, America's brooding and darkly mysterious subculture of "goths" are sometimes known in Germany as *Gruftis*—from *Gruft*, a crypt or grave.

Green Man: A Wild Man or spirit of vegetation. Though obviously pagan in origin, the Green Man is best known from his many carved portraits in English cathedrals. His face is usually composed of leaves, with more leaves and vines emerging from his mouth.

harpy: A thoroughly nasty creature of Greek mythology, having a bird's body and a woman's head. The name *harpy* comes from an ancient Greek word meaning "snatcher," referring to its habit of robbing, kidnapping, and terrorizing people with its claws.

Harudes: The first recorded tribe to occupy the Harz mountain region. Their name means "forest dwellers."

Herne the Hunter: A distinctly English figure who is still said to appear on the grounds of Windsor Castle. Like

Odin, he is the leader of the Wild Hunt, but Herne is also descended in large part from the Celtic horned god, Cernunnos. Wearing antlers and riding a horse, Herne the Hunter serves as a guardian of the forest.

hex sign: One of a variety of geometric forms drawn within a circle. Half magic, half folk art, the practice has been brought to its height by the Pennsylvania Dutch. Hex signs are painted on everything from barns to cradles to kitchen spoons to protect the home from the influence of witches.

Holda: A supernatural figure of German folk and fairytale, also spelled *Hulda*. Holda is a late expression of the Teutonic goddess Frigga. She is usually portrayed as hag. Though frightful, she is also just, rewarding the industrious and punishing the lazy. Holda is responsible for the snow, the fog, and the thunder. She also presides over the working of flax into linen and sometimes leads a procession of unbaptized souls through the sky.

Huns: A nomadic Central Asian people who made inroads into Europe in the early centuries AD and have enjoyed a very bad reputation ever since. The Huns were most likely a confederacy of tribes rather than a single ethnicity.

Imbolc: An ancient Celtic seasonal festival occurring around February 2. Celebrated today as a Wiccan sabbat, it is better known to non-Wiccans as *Candlemas, St. Brigid's Day*, or *Groundhog Day*.

intercalary days: Days inserted into a lunar or solar calendar year to reconcile that year (354 days or 365 days,

respectively) with the actual time it takes the earth to revolve around the sun (365.25 days).

Irminsul: One of several great posts or pillars erected in the German forest to represent the World Tree, known in Norse mythology as *Yggdrasill.* The most famous Irminsul stood within a sacred grove in what is now the region of Westphalia. Though destroyed by Charlemagne's army in the eighth century, the spirit of Irminsul lives on in the tradition of the Maypole. *See also* Yggdrasill.

kenning: A clever way of naming something by referring to something else. For example, a poet might say, "Sif's hair," to mean "gold," because the goddess Sif had golden hair. In order to understand the kenning, the listener had to be acquainted with, or "ken," the reference. Both Norse and Old English poets were especially fond of kennings.

kobold: A sometimes helpful, sometimes mischievous spirit that attaches itself to a household. Should the family move, the kobold will accompany them rather than stay on to haunt the old house. Kobolds are also active in mines, where their tricks can prove deadly. The German *Kobold* comes from the same root as the French-derived "goblin," but the kobold is not as consistently ugly as goblins are supposed to be. Like the dwarf, the fairy, and other Germanic sprites, the kobold is said to be about the size of a four-year-old child.

Lammas: Literally, "loaf mass." Observed on August 1 and also known as the Gule of August, Lammas celebrated the first fruits of the harvest.

mead: A mildly alcoholic beverage made from fermented honey. Mead was the preferred drink of the Vikings.

Migration Period: A time of widespread movement and resettlement of Germanic peoples occurring between 200 and 500 AD.

Nerthus: An earth goddess active in prehistoric Denmark. Sometimes equated with Freya or Freya's mother, Njord, Nerthus bestowed fertility on the fields. Her image was carried around the countryside in a cart in springtime.

Norse: Pertaining to the language, culture, and traditions of the ancient Germanic peoples of Scandinavia, especially Norway and Iceland. The Vikings were Norsemen.

Odin: Head of household of the family of gods known as the Aesir. Best known as the god of war and lord of Valhalla, Odin was also a magician, god of the dead, and retriever of the runes. He often wore a hat to disguise the fact that he had only one eye—he gave up the other in return for a drink of the mead of inspiration.

pentagram: A five-pointed star drawn with one line. The pentagram's German name, *Drudenfuss*, identifies it as the footprint of the legendary bird-footed *Drude*. The *Drudenfuss* is often found as an element of the Pennsylvania Dutch hex sign.

Perchta: *See also* Bertha.

pixie: A general term for a fairy or elf. In England, it refers to a creature that behaves much like a will-o'-the-wisp.

Purim: A festival occurring in the Jewish month of Adar, in springtime. Purim celebrates the Jewish Queen Esther's outsmarting of the evil Haman, who wanted to kill all

the Jews in Persia. Like Halloween and Walpurgis Night, Purim gives children an excuse to dress in costume, eat sweets, and make a lot of noise.

quilling: A decorative art in which narrow strips of paper are wound around a pin to make spirals, leaves, and flower petals. Quilling began as a way of using up the trimmed edges of parchment manuscript pages. The strips were originally wound around swans' feathers, or "quills."

rowan: The mountain ash, or *Pyrus aucuparia*.

Samhain: The ancient Celtic New Year's Eve, preceding the first day of the winter half of the year. Samhain is the ancestor of our Halloween.

Saxons: A Germanic people originating on the North Sea coast, where they often engaged in raiding. The Saxons were named for the short sword, or *seax*, worn by the warriors. Some Saxons, along with the Angles and Jutes, settled permanently in Britain, bringing with them an early version of the English language. Those Saxons who remained in Germany eventually made their way into the present-day states of Saxony and Saxony-Anhalt, where they were converted by the Franks and absorbed into Charlemagne's Holy Roman Empire.

Scythians: An ancient nomadic people of the Black Sea area, known for their metalworking skills.

seid: A form of divination presided over by the goddess Freya and most commonly practiced by women.

shaman: One who has undergone special initiation in order to communicate with the spirit world, usually in a trance state.

Shrove Tuesday: Also known as *Mardi Gras*, the day before Ash Wednesday when Catholics traditionally make confession and are "shriven." This is the day to use up all the butter and lard, usually by making pancakes, before the onset of the Lenten fast.

Silesia: A region of southwestern Poland, also spilling into present-day Germany and the Czech Republic. Silesia may have been named for Mount Sleza, a granite peak that was sacred to a long succession of pagan peoples in the area.

smudge stick: A tightly gathered bundle of herbs, usually sage and cedar, used by Native Americans in the Great Plains and what is now the Southwest. The smoke of the slow-burning smudge stick is used to purify spaces, people, and objects.

Song of Wayland: Old English epic poem recounting the vengeful adventures of the hamstrung Wayland the Smith.

spirit catcher: A type of amulet made in the remote district of Mustang in Nepal. Spirit catchers are constructed in the same way as the God's eyes of Mexico, though some spirit catchers are made with three sticks instead of two. Space left between the threads creates a spider-web effect. Spirit catchers are placed above the doors of houses with an array of other objects to keep witches away. Similarly, in Germany, charms to protect children were made from

nine elder twigs held together with red silk thread. *See also* God's eye.

Teutonic: A term that has come to refer to all those ruffian Germanic tribes, and their language and culture. The concept of "Teutonic" is distinct from the more northerly concept of "Norse."

Teutons: One of the first Germanic tribes to make trouble for the Romans. Originating in northern Germany and peninsular Denmark (now known as Jutland after yet another tribe, the Jutes), the Teutons spread all the way to what is now Aix-en-Provence in southeastern France, where they were broken by the Romans in 101 BCE.

Thuringia: A heavily forested region of central Germany, which the poet Goethe found almost as inspiring as the Harz. The name is the legacy of the Thuringii tribe, who first coalesced as a distinct people around 400 AD, only to be swamped by the Franks by 550.

thurse: A frost giant or ogre of Norse mythology. The thurses were the sons of the giant Ymir, having sprung from his crossed legs. The thurses were not nice and continually caused trouble for the gods.

Valhalla: "Hall of the Slain": a huge manor belonging to the god Odin, where those killed in battle were welcomed. Each morning, the warriors would fight one another to the death, as it were, only to be resurrected immediately afterward. Then, they would all sit down to second breakfast together, looking forward to another day of fighting.

Vanir: One of two families of Norse deities. The Vanir dwell in Vanheim, which was located sometimes between Asgard and the world of men and sometimes in the underworld. As gods of earth, sea, fertility, and death, the Vanir probably preceded that other family of gods, the Aesir. Subsequent intermarriage between the gods of both houses blurred the lines between the two. The goddess Freya is often counted as a member of both clans.

Volsunga Saga: Norse soap opera of epic scope. Central to the plot is the tempestuous love/hate affair between the dragon-slayer Sigurd and the Valkyrie Brynhild.

Walpurgis Night: The night of April 30, or May Eve. It is known as *Walpurgisnacht* in German, *Valborg* in Swedish, *Vappu* in Finnish, and *Čarodějnice* in Czech.

warlock: Originally, a traitor. Later, the word came to mean "wizard."

will-o'-the-wisp: Literally, "Will of the wisp": that is, a fellow named Will who carries a burning wisp of straw. Like his close cousin, Jack of the Lantern, he lures travelers off the path and into the mire. Known by many names throughout the world, this creature of ill will is a personification of the natural phosphorescence given off by rotting plant material in marshy areas. In Scandinavia, such lights were thought to be the ghosts of abandoned babies who drew the traveler to water in hopes of receiving baptism. The German *Irrlicht* (lost, wandering light) is often translated as "will-o'-the-wisp," but can also refer to the phenomenon of the anticorona that occurs in the mountains.

Wodan: Teutonic god very similar to but probably older than the Norse Odin. Principally a sky god, Wodan had a finger in just about every pot: war, magic, weather, death, and the runes. Like Odin, Wodan had a lot of nicknames and liked to disguise himself in order to travel among mortals. Wednesday is "Wodan's Day."

Yggdrasill: The World Tree of Norse mythology. An ash whose roots were watered by the Well of Wyrd, Yggdrasill's trunk extended up through the various worlds of dwarfs, elves, men, and gods. Yggdrasill means "Odin's horse," Ygg being one of the god's many names. "Odin's horse" was a kenning for gallows, alluding to the nine nights Odin spent hanging from the tree in order to acquire the runes. (Odin's actual horse was called Sleipnir.) *See also* kenning.

Bibliography

Books:

Andersen, Hans Christian. *Tales from Hans Andersen.* New York: Thomas Y. Crowell and Company (very old: no copyright or translator name).

Barber, Elizabeth Wayland. *The Mummies of Urumchi.* New York: W. W. Norton and Company, 1999.

Baroja, Julio Caro. *The World of the Witches*, translated by O. N. V. Glendinning. Chicago: University of Chicago Press, 1964.

Beckmann, Dieter, and Barbara Beckmann. *Das geheime Wissen der Kräuterhexen: Alltagswissen vergangener Zeiten.* (The Secret Knowledge of Herbal Witches: Everyday Knowledge of Bygone Times.) Munich: Deutsche Taschenbuch Verlag, 1997.

Berger, Pamela. *The Goddess Obscured.* Boston: Beacon Press, 1985.

Boyer, Marie-France. *Tree-Talk: Memories, Myths and Timeless Customs* London: Thames and Hudson, 1996.

Branston, Brian. *The Lost Gods of England*. London: Thames and Hudson, 1957.

Byock, Jesse L., trans. *The Saga of the Volsungs*. Berkeley: University of California Press, 1990.

Campbell, James Graham, et. al., eds. *Cultural Atlas of the Viking World*. Oxford, UK: Andromeda Oxford Limited, 1994.

Casanova, Gertrude. "St. Walburga," *Catholic Encyclopedia*, volume XV. New York: Robert Appleton Company, 1912.

Clarke, Susanna. *Jonathan Strange & Mr Norrell*. London: Bloomsbury, 2004.

Cooper, John Michael. *Mendelssohn, Goethe and the Walpurgis Night: The Heathen Muse in European Culture, 1700–1850*. Rochester, NY: University of Rochester Press, 2007.

Cunliffe, Barry. *Europe Between the Oceans, 9000 BC–AD 1000*. New Haven, CT: Yale University Press, 2008.

Daniels, Cora Linn, and C. M. Stevans, eds. *Encyclopedia of Superstitions, Folklore and the Occult Sciences of the World, Volume II*. Detroit, MI: Gale Research Company, 1971.

Davidson, H. R. Ellis. *Gods and Myths of Northern Europe*. Harmondsworth, UK: Penguin, 1964.

———. *Gods and Myths of the Viking Age*. New York: Bell Publishing Company, 1981.

Davidson, Hilda Ellis. *The Lost Beliefs of Northern Europe*. New York: Routledge, 1993.

Ferguson, Robert. *The Vikings: A History*. New York: Viking, 2009.

Fernández-Armesto, Felipe, ed. *The Times Guide to the Peoples of Europe*. London: Times Books, 1994.

Fischer-Fabian, S. *Die ersten Deutschen*. (The First Germans.) Bergisch Gladbach, Germany: Bastei Lübbe, 2003.

Fiske, John. *Myths and Myth-Makers : Old Tales and Superstitions Interpreted by Comparative Mythology*. Boston: Longwood Press, 1978.

Frazer, Sir James George. *The Golden Bough*, abridged edition. New York: Collier Books, 1922.

Gardner, Barbara. "Norns," in *Gods, Goddesses, and Mythology*, volume 7. Tarrytown, NY: Marshall Cavendish, 2005.

Goethe, Johann Wolfgang von. *Goethe's Faust. From the German by John Anster, LLD*. New York: Dodd, Mead and Company, 1894.

Grimm Brothers. *The German Legends of the Brothers Grimm*, edited and translated by Donald Ward. Ann Arbor: University of Michigan, Institute for the Study of Human Issues, 1981.

———. *Household Stories*. Lucy Crane, trans. New York: Dover Publications, 1963.

Grimm, Jacob. James Steven Stallybrass, trans. *Teutonic Mythology, Volumes I–III*. London: George Bell and Sons, 1883. (Republished by Dover Books, Mineola, NY, 2004.)

———. *Teutonic Mythology, Volume IV*. London: George Bell and Sons, London, 1888. (Republished by Dover Books, Mineola, NY, 2004.)

Guiley, Rosemary Ellen. *The Encyclopedia of Witches and Witchcraft, Second Edition*. New York: Checkmark Books, 1999.

Harding, Anthony. "Reformation in Barbarian Europe, 1300–600 BC," in *The Oxford Illustrated Prehistory of Europe*. New York: Oxford University Press, 1994.

"Heidenheim," in *Encyclopedia Britannica*, 15th edition. Chicago: Encyclopedia Britannica, 1980.

Herrmann, Paul. *Deutsche Mythologie*. (German Mythology.) Berlin: Aufbau Taschen Verlag, 2001.

Irwin, Kevin W. *Context and Text: Method in Liturgical Theology*. Ann Arbor: University of Michigan, Liturgical Press, 1994.

Jackson, Guida M. *Traditional Epics*. New York: Oxford University Press, 1994.

Jacob, Dorothy. *A Witch's Guide to Gardening*. New York: Taplinger Publishing Company, 1965.

Jones, Prudence, and Nigel Pennick. *A History of Pagan Europe*. New York: Routledge, 1997.

Kamm, Minnie Watson. *Old-Time Herbs for Northern Gardens*. New York: Dover Publications, 1971.

Keightley, Thomas. *The World Guide to Gnomes, Fairies, Elves, and Other Little People*. New York: Gramercy Books, 2000.

Kuhns, Elizabeth. *The Habit*. New York: Doubleday, 2003.

Lavold, Elsebeth. *Viking Patterns for Knitting*. North Pomfret, VT: Trafalgar Square Publishing, 2000.

Leach, Maria, ed. *Funk and Wagnalls Standard Dictionary of Folklore, Mythology and Legend*. New York: Funk and Wagnalls, 1949.

Leeming, David. *The Oxford Companion to World Mythology*. New York: Oxford University Press, 2005.

Lindahl, Carl, John McNamara, and John Lindow, eds. *Medieval Folklore: A Guide to Myths, Legends, Tales, Beliefs and Customs*. New York: Oxford University Press, 2002.

Magnusson, Magnus, and Hermann Palsson, trans. *Njal's Saga*. London: Penguin, 1960.

Mallory, J. P., and Victor H. Mair. *The Tarim Mummies: Ancient China and the Mystery of the Earliest Peoples from the West*. London: Thames and Hudson, 2000.

Maple, Eric. *The Dark World of Witches*. New York: A. S. Barnes and Company, 1964.

Mercatante, Anthony S. *The Magic Garden*. New York: Harper and Row, 1976.

Metzger, Christine, ed. *Culinaria Germany*. Cologne, Germany: Könemann, 2000.

Ott, Michael T. "Oil of Saints," in *The Catholic Encyclopedia*, volume XI. New York: Robert Appleton Company, 1911.

Petzoldt, Leander. "Spirits and Ghosts," in Carl Lindahl et al, eds., *Medieval Folklore*. Oxford: Oxford University Press, 2002.

Pickering, David. *Cassell's Dictionary of Superstitions*. London: Cassell, 2002.

Porteous, Alexander. *The Forest in Folklore and Mythology*. New York: Macmillan, 1928.

Preussler, Otfried. *The Little Witch*. Anthea Bell, trans. New York: Abelard-Schumann, 1969.

Rätsch, Christian. *Walpurgisnacht: Von fliegenden Hexen und ekstatischen Tänzen*. (Walpurgis Night: Of Flying Witches and Ecstatic Dances.) Munich: AT Verlag, 2007.

Rausch, Andrea, and Brigitte Lotz. *Dumont's Lexicon of Herbs*. Lisse, the Netherlands: Rebo Publishers, 2004.

Redlich, H. V. "St. Walburga of Heidenheim," in *New Catholic Encyclopedia*. Washington, DC: The Catholic University of America, 1967.

———. "Walburga of Heidenheim," in *New Catholic Encyclopedia*, second edition, volume 14. Detroit, MI: Gale Research Company, 2003.

Robinson, Orrin W. *Old English and Its Closest Relatives*. Stanford, CA: Stanford University Press, 1992.

Russ, Jennifer M. *German Festivals and Customs*. London: Oswald Wolff, 1982.

Russell, Jeffrey B., and Brooks Alexander. *A History of Witchcraft: Sorcerers, Heretics and Pagans*. London: Thames & Hudson, 2007.

Sanders, Jack. *Hedgemaids and Fairy Candles: The Lives and Lore of North American Wildflowers*. Camden, ME: Ragged Mountain Press, 1993.

Santino, Jack. *Halloween and Other Festivals of Life and Death*. Knoxville: University of Tennessee Press, 1994.

Scherf, Gertrud. *Zauberpflanzen, Hexenkräuter: Mythos und Magie heimischer Wild- und Kulturpflanzen.* (Enchanted Plants, Witches' Herbs: Myth and Magic of Indigenous Wild and Cultivated Plants.) Munich: BLV, 2003.

Seymour, John. *The Forgotten Arts and Crafts.* New York: Dorling Kindersley, 2001.

Steiger, Brad. *Real Ghosts, Restless Spirits and Haunted Places.* Detroit, MI: Visible Ink, 2003.

Stock, Lorraine K. "Wild Woman," in Carl Lindahl et al., eds., *Medieval Folklore.* Oxford: Oxford University Press, 2002.

Sturluson, Snorri. *Heimskringla: or, Lives of the Norse Kings.* Mineola, NY: Dover Publications, 1990.

———. Translated by Jean I. Young, Jon Thorisson, ed. *The Viking Gods.* Reykjavik, Iceland: Gudrun, 1995.

Summers, Montague. *The Geography of Witchcraft.* New York: University Books, 1958.

Talbot, Rob, and Robin Whiteman. *Brother Cadfael's Herb Garden: An Illustrated Companion to Medieval Plants and Their Uses.* New York: Little, Brown and Company, 1997.

Thompson, Sue Ellen. *Holiday Symbols*, second edition. Detroit, MI: Omnigraphics, 2000.

Thonger, Richard. *A Calendar of German Customs.* Chester Springs, PA: Dufour Editions, 1968. (Originally published by Oswald Wolff [publishing], Munich, 1966.)

Thorsson, Ornolfur, ed. *The Sagas of Icelanders: A Selection.* New York: Viking, 1997.

Todd, Malcolm. *The Early Germans*, second edition. Malden, MA: Blackwell Publishing, 2004.

———. *Everyday Life of the Barbarians: Goths, Franks and Vandals*. New York: G. P. Putnam's Sons, 1972.

Turner, Patricia, and Charles Russell Coulter. *The Dictionary of Ancient Deities*. New York: Oxford University Press, 2000.

Wilbur, C. Keith. *Indian Handicrafts*. Chester, CT: The Globe Pequot Press, 1990.

Woll, Johanna. *Feste und Bräuche im Jahreslauf*. (Festivals and Customs throughout the Year.) Stuttgart, Germany: Ulmer, 2001.

Other:

Ashliman, D. L. "Witchcraft Legends," www.pitt.edu/~dash/witch.html.

Borden, Adrienne, and Steve Coyote. "The Smudging Ceremony," in *Shaman's Drum*, Spring 1987.

Cramer, Anna. "The World Is a Disk: The Sky of Nebra—Germany's 3,600-Year-Old Astronomical Clock," *German Life*, February/March 2008.

Dashu, Max. "Kings Against Witches. Excerpt from the *Secret History of the Witches*," www.suppressedhistories.net/secret_history/kings_witches.html (2000).

Die Benediktinerinnenabtei St. Walburg. "Heilige Walburga—Leben und Wirken" (Life and Work of the Holy Walburga), http://www.abtei-st-walburg.de/heilige-walburga/.

Dorn, Stefanie. "Walpurgisnacht im Harz: Hexenzauber und Liebesorakel. Führerscheinprüfung für Hexenbesen" (Walpurgis Night in the Harz: Witches' Spells and Love Divination. Driving Test for Witches' Brooms), http://archiv.rhein-zeitung.de/on/97/04/23/topnews/walpurgis.html. (Article first appeared in the newspaper *Rhein-Zeitung*, of Koblenz, Germany, on April 23, 1997.)

FinnGuide. "May Day, Labour Day," www.finnguide.fi/calendarevents.asp?month=5&p=33.

Fish Eaters. "Walpurgisnacht," http://www.fisheaters.com/walpurgisnacht.html.

Harvey, Steenie. "Season of the Witch: Walpurgisnacht in Germany's Harz Mountains," www.worldandi.com/specialreport/walpu/walpu.html.

———. "Walpurgisnacht: Shrieks and Spooks in Schierke," *German Life*, April/May 2000, 24.

Hodge, Winifred. "Waelburga and the Rites of May," www.friggasweb.org.

Johnston, Rosie. "Czechs celebrate 'Čarodějnice'—An Annual Witch-Burning Festival," *Radio Prague Magazine* archive, http://www.radio.cz/en/section/curraffrs/czechs-celebrate-carodejnice-an-annual-witch-burning-festival (May 2, 2008).

Jones, Terry H. "Saint Walburga," http://saints.sqpn.com/saint-walburga/.

Kubik, Libor. "Czech—Witches—Accident," *Radio Prague E-News*, http://archiv.radio.cz/news/GB/2000/02.05.html (May 2, 2000).

Lazarová, Daniela. "Witch-Burning Night Brings Record Number of Fires," *Radio Prague News* archive, http://www.radio.cz/en/news/90914 (May 1, 2007).

———. "Magazine," *Radio Prague News* archive, http://www.radio.cz/en/section/magazine/magazine-2006-04-29 (April 29, 2006).

———. "Magazine," *Radio Prague News* archive, http://www.radio.cz/en/section/magazine/magazine-2007-05-05 (May 5, 2007).

Lendering, Jona. "Nehalennia," Online at http://www.livius.org/ne-nn/nehalennia/nehalennia.html. © Jona Lendering for Livius.Org, 2002.

Luleå University (Sweden). " 'Pask'—Easter," www.luth.se/luth/present/sweden/history/folklore/easter.html.

Mapes, Terri. "Walpurgis Night in Sweden: Sweden's Walpurgis Tradition," http://goscandinavia.about.com/od/annualeventstraditions/qt/walpurgisnight.htm (About.com).

myCzechRepublic. "The Burning of the Witches, April 30," www.myczechrepublic.com/czech_holidays/burning-witches.html.

Oberwesel.de. "Wine-Witch-Night," http://oberwesel.de/portal/index.php?option=com_content&task=view&id=484&lang=english. © 2010 Oberwesel Stadt der Türme und des Weines.

Ogilvie, Astrid E. J., and Gísli Pálsson. "Weather and Witchcraft in the Sagas of Icelanders," www.dur.ac.uk/medieval.www/sagaconf/ogilvie.htm.

Prague TV. "Witches' Night," http://prague.tv/articles/visitors-guide/witches-night (April 26, 2006).

Schulte-Peevers, Andrea. "Witches, Trains and Half Timber—The Magic of the Harz," *German Life*, April/May, 1996, 34.

Skott, Fredrik. "Easter Witches in Sweden," presented at a symposium on "Traditional Masks and Mumming in Northern Europe," August 2002. (Also published with Terry Gunnell, ed., Uppsala, Sweden, 2007.) PDF available online at www.fredrikskott.se/EasterWitches.pdf.

Weinhexenmahl.de. "Wein-Hexennacht in Oberwesel am Rhein" (Wine-Witch Night in Oberwesel am Rhein), www.weinhexenmahl.de/.

Index

To Write to the Author

If you wish to contact the author or would like more information about this book, please write to the author in care of Llewellyn Worldwide, and we will forward your request. Both the author and the publisher appreciate hearing from you and learning of your enjoyment of this book and how it has helped you. Llewellyn Worldwide cannot guarantee that every letter written to the author can be answered, but all will be forwarded. Please write to:

Linda Raedisch
℅ Llewellyn Worldwide
2143 Wooddale Drive
Woodbury, MN 55125-2989

Please enclose a self-addressed stamped envelope for reply, or $1.00 to cover costs. If outside the USA, enclose an international postal reply coupon.